FOREIGN DIRECT INVESTMENT IN THE 1990s
A NEW CLIMATE IN THE THIRD WORLD

FOREIGN DIRECT INVESTMENT IN THE 1990s

A NEW CLIMATE IN THE THIRD WORLD

by

Cynthia Day Wallace
and contributors

Foreword by Murray Weidenbaum

MARTINUS NIJHOFF PUBLISHERS

DORDRECHT / BOSTON / LONDON

ISBN 0-7923-0572-8

Published by Martinus Nijhoff Publishers,
P.O. Box 163, 3300 AD Dordrecht, The Netherlands.

Sold and distributed in the U.S.A. and Canada
by Kluwer Academic Publishers,
101 Philip Drive, Norwell, MA 02061, U.S.A.

In all other countries, sold and distributed
by Kluwer Academic Publishers Group,
P.O. Box 322, 3300 AH Dordrecht, The Netherlands.

printed on acid free paper

Cover design by C. D. Wallace

Printed in the Netherlands

TABLE OF CONTENTS

ACKNOWLEDGEMENTS

A genuine expression of thanks goes to each of the contributing authors for their response and cooperation at all stages of the editorial process. Additional thanks goes to Don Guertin, former Exxon executive, for his excellent input on the formulation of the corporate questionnaire, and to Wingate Lloyd of ITT, Harvey Bale of the Pharmaceutical Manufacturers Association, and Detlev Vagts of Harvard Law and Business Schools for their helpful comments and insights leading to its finalization.

CSIS interns Mitch Brahin, Kate Goralski, and Mark Whitmore earn kudos for working tirelessly on administrative and technical aspects of the questionnaire process—from cross-listing corporate compilations to registering survey data and making follow-up calls. Mark Nolan also lent his expertise and insights in computer techniques and corporate savvy. Mary Marik pitched in and worked miracles with my manuscript which none other than Mary could possibly have deciphered, replete with manifold arrows and asterisks which only she can bring into the desired sequence. Special acknowledgement goes to intern Andrew Jones, without whose outstanding assistance and diligence in the preparation of graphs and analytical data, this task would have been monumentally hindered.

My gratitude is extended to the Richard Lounsbery Foundation—especially Director Fred Seitz who conveyed his interest in the project to Foundation President, Alan McHenry—and to the Agency for International Development—especially Michael Unger who brought the project to the attention of AID Administrator Peter McPherson and to his colleague Ken Kauffman—for their faithful and generous support of this phase of the project.

FOREWORD

For too long, the literature on the relationships between advanced and developing nations has been filled with sensational charges of imperialism, economic aggression, and similar stereotypes. In this book, Dr. Cynthia Wallace and her associates have filled a long-felt need. Their eight essays, in the aggregate, provide a scholarly and more positive analysis of the role of foreign direct investment in Third World nations.

This book provides a desirable sense of balance to the public debate by dealing with the concerns of both the host government and the "foreign" private business. Individual chapters go beyond the broad issues to tackle such specific questions as the form of investment agreements and the ways in which to increase the efficiency of international trade, and to identify the indirect and hidden barriers to commerce between the developing and advanced economies.

We can hope that this book lowers the decibel level characteristic of current discussions involving the emerging relationships between the developed nations and those that seek to join that category. There are of course difficult problems to be dealt with in the area of business-government relations within a single country. Consider the tremendous amount of resources that a typical U.S. corporation devotes to dealing with the host of Federal government regulatory agencies and an equal or greater number of Congressional committees and subcommittees—plus a substantial number of state and local government departments that impinge in one way or another on the decision-making of the individual enterprise.

Clearly, a transnational enterprise and a foreign host government, it should be anticipated, will encounter a far greater array of obstacles and difficulties in their paths. The sensible approach, it would seem, is to face each of these problem areas in a straightforward manner.

Essentially, this is the task to which the authors of this book have set themselves, to begin to articulate the kinds of public sector and private sector decisions that are involved in promoting a greater participation of private enterprise in the economic development of the Third World.

This approach is a useful antidote to the usual preoccupations with the "imperialistic aggrandizement" view of business firms in the Third World. The cynic in me wonders to what extent the antipathy often expressed toward the larger transnational enterprises occurs because they are the major—and usually more efficient—alternative to direct governmental control and operation of the economic development process. We must wonder whether businesses are singled out because they pose a real threat to the establishment and maintenance of concentrated economic power in government.

It can hardly be a coincidence that those Third World nations who have given the widest scope to private enterprise have made the most rapid progress in their economic development. The contrast between the market-oriented economies of South Korea, Taiwan, Singapore, and Hong Kong are in striking contrast with the socialized economies of North Korea and China.

Some understanding, however, of the concerns of the people and governments in the Third World can be gained by examining the current adverse reactions in many parts of the United States to the accelerated inflow of direct foreign investment. The argument is all too familiar. The uninformed reaction to foreigners "buying up America" at times approaches near hysteria. The United States is "losing control" of its economic destiny and is in danger of becoming a wholly-owned subsidiary of "Japan, Inc."

Although the facts show that foreign direct investment is a minute factor in the American economy, perceptions are otherwise and sensibilities must be taken into account. The point to be made seems quite clear: if the people in a strong, advanced country can raise flags of caution in the face of rising foreign investment, it is likely that the concerns of citizens of the Third World will be greater.

To some extent, the initial hostility may be generated by local companies that fear new and likely stronger competition. Recall the wave of concern in France a decade or two ago about the potential "cocacolanization" of that country. In practice, U.S. direct foreign investment contributed to the rebuilding of the French economy into an effective world-wide competitor. The moral of the tale should be evident.

Murray Weidenbaum

INTRODUCTION

Foreign direct investment (FDI) has assumed renewed prominence and is demanding urgent attention on the U.S. and international economic agenda. It is doing so against the background of rapid integration of world financial markets and striking shifts in the direction of trade and investment flows.

This volume represents one phase of a major initiative conducted by the author/editor, at the Center for Strategic and International Studies, to investigate and assess the most urgent aspects of both Third World and industrialized country developments in this increasingly strategic area of economic activity. The phase presented here focuses on the Third World as a critical component in this global process.

A sense of the need to review U.S. international investment policy and U.S. corporate interests and strategy in the Third World emerged out of discussions in the context of an 18-month, high level task-force study conducted in 1985-1987 at CSIS, reassessing U.S. overall economic policy and strategy. The results appear in the volume, *Keeping Pace: U.S. Policies and Global Economic Change.*

The present volume follows up on some of the issues identified in the task-force study, by investigating the various impediments to the free flow of direct investment in developing nations, including the ways in which these impact on the implementation of U.S. policy objectives.

For example, if the administration wants our major industrialized trading partners to assume a greater role in equalizing the burden-sharing with regard to Third World economic strains, it needs to ensure that our own policies (of protection and promotion of FDI) are clearly articulated. If we deem that FDI can indeed play a role in the economic growth of debt-burdened Third World nations, we need to target the obstacles actually confronted in the course of international business

---

* For the FDI issues, see "Foreign Direct Investment: A New Climate for Negotiations with the Third World", by Cynthia Day Wallace, chapter 8 in Yochelson, ed., *Keeping Pace: U.S. Policies and Global Economic Change,* Cambridge, Ballinger, 1988.

operations. We need to formulate an approach that will minimize such impediments to mutually beneficial FDI activity and to assess the most effective way of promoting and protecting FDI in cases where the incentives of the host country itself are not adequate to attract the needed investment.

Are government initiatives what are needed, or is the private sector the sole appropriate catalyst here? Should solutions be based on normal business criteria exclusively, or are these at odds with our overall national interests?

If government has a role, should it aim for unilateral, bilateral, or multilateral solutions? Or should we look for a combination of the above?

These and related questions have been considered through an examination of innovative approaches to FDI, including the increasing variety of debt-equity swap schemes as means of acquiring investment facilities. Some of the more recent unilateral, bilateral and multilateral promotion and protection schemes are evaluated in an effort to guage the viability of these various initiatives, and to determine which of them are worthy of supportive action by the U.S. government and its agencies.

There is an urgent need to clarify the interests of U.S. government and business, with regard to FDI, in the changed global economic environment. There is a need to reassess the degree to which the U.S. government should concern itself with the international business activities of the private sector to ensure those interests, and the degree to which it should adopt a laissez-faire policy vis-a-vis American corporations operating abroad.

There is a need as well to evaluate the role of FDI in Third World countries as a boost to economic growth and infrastructure development. The corollary here is the extent to which U.S. corporations should be encouraged—if at all—by the U.S. government, in view of the globally reciprocal effects of economic well-being, to invest in regions that would not otherwise attract FDI, either on their own merits or by virtue of such incentives as might be offered by the host.

The present analysis concentrates on the new Third World investment climate, with particular emphasis on the need to accelerate foreign capital flows to these nations as an impetus to their urgently needed economic growth. The investigation seeks to go beyond the restraints posed by host state regulations and administrative policies, to identify the various difficulties that can result from capital market infrastructures, exchange rate fluctuations, exchange controls, industrial policies, anti-competitive corporate behavior, and other restraining influences beyond pure law and administrative policy. The study considers how U.S. policy—including current and projected bilateral and multilateral initiatives—can best facilitate the free flow of investment capital.

This volume represents a cross-section of views from the political, financial, legal, academic and business communities.

Specialists in the various aspects of FDI were carefully selected and invited to address specific issues identified with their respective areas of competence. The experts collaborating in this study are Harvey E. Bale, Senior Vice President of the Pharmaceutical Manufacturers Association; Rimmer de Vries, Senior Vice President and Chief Economist of Morgan Guaranty Trust; Clarke N. Ellis, Director of the Office of Economic Policy in the Bureau of East Asian and Pacific Affairs at the State Department; Donald L. Guertin, Senior Research Fellow and Director for the Atlantic Council and member of the Business Roundtable; Theodore H. Moran, Professor and Director of International Business Diplomacy at the School of Foreign Service of Georgetown University; Charles S. Pearson, Professor of International Economics at the School of Advanced International Studies (SAIS) of Johns Hopkins University; and Detlev F. Vagts, Professor of International Law at Harvard Law School.

Clarke Ellis, with his lengthy service in government, and Don Guertin, offering a long association with international business, were invited to address the ways in which FDI in the Third World can be promoted and facilitated without engendering market-distortive side effects or increasing unnecessary governmental intervention in MNE operations. Don Guertin, who has worked extensively in this area, was particularly encouraged to address, in his analysis, what form an investment agreement should take (code or treaty; multilateral or bilateral) and what items should be contained in the provisions to best embody a regional or global political consensus on increased investment protection and reduced government intervention in FDI flows. Clarke Ellis, having dealt with investment issues in the State Department for many years, was asked to concentrate on how the U.S. leadership role can most effectively be exercised to orchestrate a coordinated investment policy with our major industrialized trading partners and to induce them to share in the effort to foster sustained economic growth in the Third World.

Harvey Bale, with reference to his own policymaking past, was asked to participate in the U.S. leadership role discussion, along with Clark Ellis. In particular, in consideration of his personal involvement in the Uruguay Round of GATT negotiations, Bale was asked to discuss how performance requirements can best be diminished to minimize distortive effects on international trade flows and to encourage foreign investors to enter Third World markets.

Ted Moran and Charles Pearson, also involved in policy formulation through international business diplomacy, were invited to contribute their views to the discussion on trade-related investment performance requirements from their vast and scholarly research on this timely topic.

Detlev Vagts was looked to in his capacity as international lawyer to elaborate, along with the question of international agreements, on how protection can best be afforded and maintained for both corporate investor and host government, as well as for the home state, with guarantees that are reliable and adequately enforceable.

Rimmer de Vries, having distinguished himself as an international economist in the complex world of international finance, was invited to clarify for us some of the extra-legal, extra-political, and less easily identifiable barriers to Third World direct investment posed by host capital market infrastructures, exchange rate fluctuations, exchange controls, and other realities of international financial interaction. He was also requested to elaborate on debt-equity swaps and other innovative schemes for dealing with Third World debt by various forms of direct investment.

With the participation of all the above, both U.S. government and private sector interests have been comprehensively if not exhaustively addressed. Along with our global leadership responsibilities in assisting depressed free-market economies, special attention was accorded the private sector whose particular views were solicited by means of a confidential questionnaire geared to assure that corporations' most critical concerns would be adequately represented.

The concluding chapter, prepared by the editor, presents the results of the corporate survey on MNE/host relations conducted on the basis of the questionnaire. Where appropriate, various authors' observations are drawn in to supplement or shed further light on survey findings. The survey serves to highlight certain risks and difficulties actually encountered in entering Third World markets, or in day-to-day operations, once an enterprise is established in the host country. It also identifies the major impediments to the free flow of investment capital and the ways in which U.S. policy may foster or, alternatively, hinder American FDI in developing nations.

Cynthia Day Wallace

I. FOREIGN DIRECT INVESTMENT AND INTERNATIONAL CAPITAL FLOWS TO THIRD WORLD NATIONS: UNITED STATES POLICY CONSIDERATIONS

By Clarke N. Ellis[*]

Introduction

> [Foreign capital] instead of being viewed as a rival ought to be considered as a most valuable auxiliary, conducing to put in motion a greater quantity of productive labor and a greater portion of useful enterprise than could exist without it.
> — Alexander Hamilton[1]

The above quotation, made by the first finance minister of a newly independent developing country nearly two centuries ago, provides a succinct statement of the benefits of foreign direct investment. The cabinet officer was Treasury Secretary Alexander Hamilton and the developing country was the United States. The open policy toward foreign investment advocated by Hamilton has guided the United States through most of our history and with positive results for our economic development.

Attitudes toward foreign investment have not been uniformly positive, however, in either developing or developed countries. The 1960s and 1970s were periods during which foreign investment and

---

[*] The author is currently Director of the Office of Economic Policy of the Bureau of East Asian and Pacific Affairs, Department of State. He was Director of the Office of Investment Affairs, Department of State, from July 1984 to August 1987. The views expressed by the author do not necessarily represent those of the Department of State.

1 Quoted in Sidney E. Rolfe and Walter Damm, eds., *The Multinational Corporation in the World Economy* (New York: Praeger Publishers, 1970), p. 121.

1

multinational corporations (MNCs)[1] were considered threats to national sovereignty and economic development. Even popular book titles of the period conveyed the mood:[2] *Global Reach, Sovereignty at Bay* and *The American Challenge*. They give a flavor of the suspicion that existed.[3] This was the period of the Congressional hearings into the activities of ITT in Chile, the launching of the U.N. Commission on Transnational Corporations and the initiation of negotiations of several codes of conduct aimed at regulating the activities of MNCs. International business was clearly on the defensive.

Today, at the end of the 1980s, the situation is quite different, and widespread agreement exists that foreign investment is beneficial. Within the last few years, Marxist governments, including the Soviet Union, the People's Republic of China, and even the Socialist Republic of Vietnam, have promulgated new foreign investment laws aimed at attracting foreign capital and technology, and the Soviet Union has recently talked about negotiating investment protection agreements.[4] Attendees at a UN sponsored high-level Roundtable on the UN Code of Conduct on Transnational Corporations in Montreux, Switzerland in October 1986, including two communist and nine third world representatives, unanimously concluded that:

> transnational corporations, in pursuing their economic objectives, can make a contribution to the development process by providing capital, technology, managerial resources and markets.[5]

---

[1]In this paper the terms multinational corporation (MNC), transnational corporation (TNC) and multinational enterprise (MNE) are used without distinction.

[2]Richard J. Barnet and Ronald E. Muller, *Global Reach* (New York: Simon and Schuster, 1974); Raymond Vernon, *Sovereignty at Bay: The Multinational Spread of U.S. Enterprises,* (New York: Basic Books, Inc., 1971); and J.-J. Servan-Schreiber, *The American Challenge* (New York: Avon Books, 1969).

[3] A summary of these concerns is contained in Clarke N. Ellis, "United States Multinational Corporations: The Impact of Foreign Direct Investment on United States Foreign Relations," 11 *The San Diego Law Review* (November 1973), pp. 1-26.

[4]Foreign Broadcast Information Service (FBIS), January 19, 1988, reporting a TASS English-language broadcast of January 18, 1988.

[5]The United Nations Centre on Transnational Corporations, "The Code: High-level Roundtable on the Code," *The CTC Reporter*, No. 22 (Autumn 1986), p. 9

The task for policymakers today—including those in the United States—is to examine ways of increasing foreign investment flows, especially to the developing countries (LDCs).

This chapter first examines briefly why this change in attitude toward foreign direct investment has occurred. It then summarizes U.S. policy toward direct investment in the LDCs. The main part of the analysis looks at the primary obstacles to increasing foreign investment in the LDCs and what is being done, and might be done, in terms of U.S. policy to overcome them. Finally, an effort is made to draw some conclusions for U.S. policy.

Foreign Investment in LDCs in the 1980s

Given the controversy associated with foreign investment in the LDCs in the 1960s and 1970s, the generally positive attitude in the 1980s seems at first surprising, but in fact is readily explainable. One reason is that foreign investors have, in many cases, become better corporate citizens. The several general and specific codes of conduct for MNCs developed to date have had important influences as levers on— and guidance for—MNC conduct.[1] These include the 1976 OECD Guidelines for Multinational Enterprises, the 1977 ILO Tripartite Declaration of Principles Concerning Multinational Enterprises and Social Policy, and the more specialized 1980 UNCTAD code entitled, The Set of Multilaterally Agreed Equitable Principles and Rules for the Control of Restrictive Business Practices.

Although the decade-long efforts in the UN Commission on Transnational Corporations to draft a code have not been crowned with success, the extensive discussions on corporate behavior and government responsibilities to foreign investors have, in this writer's view, contributed to the more positive environment for international business. Moreover, stung by the criticisms of inappropriate MNC activities in a number of countries, the international business community has made considerable efforts of its own to set standards for acceptable international business behavior and corporate good citizenship. These include the 1972 Guidelines for International Investment of the

---

1John M. Kline, *International Codes and Multinational Business* (Westport, Connecticut: Quorum Books, 1985), pp. 76-87.

3

International Chamber of Commerce (ICC) and a host of industry-wide and individual corporate codes of conduct.[1]

In addition to changes in corporate behavior, international corporations have shown increased flexibility concerning the form of their business activity abroad. This includes a greater willingness, in some cases, to accept innovative arrangements such as joint ventures, turnkey projects, build-own-transfer (BOT) arrangements and licensing agreements rather than the traditional wholly-owned subsidiary.

A second explanation for the more positive attitude toward foreign investment is that host governments in developing countries have become more confident in dealing with MNCs. Over the years, LDC governments have gained considerable experience and been able to share that experience. Bilateral and multilateral assistance programs have helped LDC governments to develop their administrative infrastructure and body of laws and regulations to deal with foreign investment problems. In the case of the UN Centre on Transnational Corporations this has even involved advising LDC governments on negotiations with MNCs.

Probably the most important reason for today's more positive environment toward foreign investment is economic necessity. The 1970s were boom times for not only petroleum producing LDCs but also for producers of many other commodities. The prospect of ever-increasing oil prices and high world-wide inflation convinced many LDCs that they could easily borrow their way to development and pay off their debts in depreciated dollars. The internationally active commercial banks, flush with the surpluses of the OPEC nations, were only too happy to recycle the petrodollars to the developing nations.

By the early 1980s, the situation had drastically changed. The peak for petroleum prices was reached in 1981 and by 1986 had fallen by about two-thirds before recovering slightly in 1987. The severe recession in the United States and most other industrialized countries starting in 1982 broke the back of inflation in the developed world and lessened their demand for LDC oil, commodities and other exports. Beginning with Mexico in 1982, many LDCs of all stages of development—and many communist nations—have experienced severe problems in servicing their huge external debt. In turn, their credit problems have made it much more difficult than in the preceding decade to finance development through debt. This situation has

---

[1]Kline, pp. 89-98.

sparked new interest on the part of many countries in foreign direct investment as an alternative source of capital and technology.

The need is clear. Net financial flows to the developing countries have dropped considerably since 1982. International bank lending as a percentage of net financial flows to developing countries fell from an annual average of almost 36 percent over the 1978-1982 period, to only 19 percent during 1983-1986. Foreign direct investment flows to the LDCs over the same two periods held steady at an average of 11 percent of total net flows. In dollar amounts, however, foreign direct investment flows to the LDCs fell from an annual average of $13 billion in 1978-1982 to less than $10 billion during 1983-1986.[1] Also significant is the fact that LDCs played host to almost 31 percent of the world stock of foreign direct investment in 1967 but only about 23 percent in 1986.[2] The question thus arises whether or not foreign direct investment—if given the appropriate economic and political environment—could play a larger role in LDC development than is currently the case.

U.S. Policy Toward Foreign Investment in the LDCs

As noted at the beginning of this chapter, the United States has long recognized the economic benefits to be had from foreign investment. The most recent comprehensive rendering of our international investment policy was contained in a statement issued by President Ronald Reagan on September 9, 1983.[3] That statement:

— reaffirmed the fundamental premise of U.S. policy that "foreign investment flows which respond to private market forces will lead to more efficient international production and thereby benefit both home and host countries";

---

[1] Statistics derived from unpublished figures compiled by the Development Assistance Committee of the Organization for Economic Cooperation and Development (Paris: OECD, 1988).

[2] U.S. Department of Commerce, *Direct Investment Update: Trends in International Direct Investment,* (Staff report prepared by John Rutter, Investment Research Division, International Trade Administration Washington, D.C.: USDOC, 1988).

[3] Ronald Reagan, "International Investment Policy Statement" (Washington, D.C.: The White House, September 9, 1983).

— expressed our strong support for the fair, equitable and nondiscriminatory treatment of foreign investment in accordance with the standards of international law; and
— registered our concern with the increased use of governmental measures designed to distort or impede international investment flows.

At the same time, the statement also recognized the special need to increase investment flows to developing countries through both bilateral and multilateral programs. This constitutes an exception to the general U.S. policy principle that investment flows should respond to market forces and that governments should be basically neutral. Before discussing how the United States can best contribute to increasing equity flows to the LDCs within the context of its overall policy on international investment, it is necessary to turn briefly to the economic and political obstacles to investment that MNCs encounter in the developing world.

Obstacles to Foreign Investment in the LDCs

Economic obstacles include the general state of the international economy, technological change, and structural and cultural factors in the host country. An individual host country can do little to affect major developments in the world economy which in turn can have a major influence on investment flows. Recession or sluggish growth in the developed countries tends to dampen the interest in export-oriented investment in the LDCs. New inventions and the development of synthetics may make some LDC products obsolete; medical research may lessen demand for others (for example, worries about the health effects of caffeine, tobacco and saturated fats); and new technologies may work to lessen the traditional LDC advantage in labor intensive products. The latter is a growing problem as robotics and information processing technology alter the nature of the workplace.

Structural obstacles to investment include the host country's location, size, resource endowment, institutions and infrastructure. In the short run, most are not susceptible to change. A country without natural resources and a small domestic market is not going to be able to attract foreign investment unless, like Hong Kong and Singapore, it possesses exceptional human capital and a commercially strategic location.

The absence of the necessary modern infrastructure is also a deterrent to investment. Transportation and communications facilities, reliable public utilities and qualified local laborers, managers and government officials are obvious elements in an infrastructure that an investor will seek. The availability of foreign exchange, a functioning local capital market, and reliable locally-sourced inputs are also important.

Closely related to the problems of inadequate infrastructure are cultural impediments to investment. In fact, the lack of infrastructure may at least in part result from cultural reasons. Risk-averting traditional societies may emphasize family and communal values and discourage entrepreneurial activity and education in modern commercial and technical fields.

Political obstacles to foreign investment in developing countries can be grouped under the general headings of uncertainty, statist outlook of host governments, and discrimination.

Uncertainty with regard to the political situation and the rules of the game for investors is frequently cited by MNCs as a reason for staying out of or not increasing their involvement in a particular country. Political instability due to insurgency and actual or threatened hostilities with neighbors are obvious negative factors. Sharp national divisions on the issue of foreign investment, which could lead to major changes in the treatment of foreign investment in the event of a change in government, can also be an obstacle even without violence because investors base investment decisions on future business expectations. Ironically, a restrictive but stable investment climate may not deter an MNC if it has found a profit-making opportunity, while an investment environment that is in flux but generally improving may encourage an enterprise to delay investing in the hopes of getting a better deal later on.

The statist outlook of host governments can be an important obstacle to investors. To some extent this is unavoidable because national governments and increasingly globally oriented corporations have different perspectives. What national government officials regard as foreign investment is very much internal from the point of view of multinational business executives. Profit-maximizing investment, production and marketing strategies of a truly multinational enterprise may conflict with the growth, employment and other economic objectives of the governments of the countries in which it operates. In

7

the extreme case, governments may levy conflicting requirements on such firms, as has been the case in divergent export control laws.

More relevant to the present analysis is the general non-market attitude of many LDC governments. Such governments sometimes consider private foreign investment a form of foreign aid. They expect the MNC to contribute capital, technology, employment and foreign exchange without taking into account the private investor's need to make a profit, to be able to realize that profit in convertible form, and to receive protection for his intellectual property such as patents, trademarks and copyrights. In order to achieve certain national goals, governments may try to impose performance requirements on MNCs as a condition for approving their investments. Performance requirements include:

a) local content requirements,
b) export performance requirements,
c) trade balancing requirements,
d) technology transfer and licensing requirements,
e) exchange and remittance restrictions,
f) domestic sales requirements,
g) local equity requirements,
h) product mandating requirements and
i) manufacturing requirements and limitations.

Since these measures may serve to discourage potential investors, governments often seek to offset them by offering MNCs incentives in the form of tax breaks, outright grants, infrastructure, tariff protection and other benefits. The net result may be to restrict or distort trade as well as investment flows and to reduce the benefits of foreign investment to the LDCs.

Additional obstacles frequently associated with a statist approach are excessive government involvement in the economy, bureaucratic red tape—which often encourages corruption as a means of avoiding it—and a lack of transparency regarding rules and regulations. The ultimate gesture of the statist approach vis-a-vis a foreign investor is, of course, expropriation.

A number of political impediments to investment can be lumped together as discriminatory practices. Discrimination may have several origins including nationalism, ethnic bias and favoritism for host government-owned enterprises or local firms. Discrimination may take the form of exclusion from certain sectors; unequal application of the performance requirements noted above; and denial of national treatment with respect to eligibility for government loans and subsidies, access to local credit markets, taxation and ability to compete for host government procurement.

Overcoming the Obstacles to Investment in the LDCs

What are the most effective means to overcome the obstacles described above and facilitate foreign investment in the LDCs? How can U.S. leadership best be exercised to achieve this result? This chapter deals with these questions by examining what the United States is doing unilaterally, bilaterally and multilaterally.

Overcoming Economic Obstacles

Consistent with its free-market orientation, the United States as a general rule should not try to encourage investment in the LDCs that does not make long-term economic sense. "Hot-house" foreign investment projects created for political reasons with subsidies from developed country governments and high tariff walls in the host country can produce inefficient allocations of scarce resources, distortions in trade flows and give rise to charges in the home country that foreign investment exports jobs. Although the U.S. economy appears to remain strong at the moment, a renewed downturn could bring attacks on foreign investment as it has in previous recessions.

What governments and international organizations can do is to assist in building the infrastructure—physical, human and institutional—necessary to attract foreign investment and to stimulate the development of the local private sector. Recognizing the development role of trade and investment, the U.S. Agency for International Development (AID) has begun to shift the emphasis of its programs in many countries to meet these objectives. The establishment of the Private Enterprise Bureau in AID is just one example.

Despite this general presumption in favor of market forces, the U.S. Government and U.S. supported international organizations have found it appropriate to intervene more directly in the investment process in some instances. For example, there may be a lack of information about investment opportunities, or direct financing may be necessary to act as a catalyst to investment.

The Overseas Private Investment Corporation (OPIC) is a U.S. government controlled corporation whose main purpose (discussed below) is to provide political risk insurance for U.S. investment in over 100 LDCs. It also provides a limited amount of direct financing, typically for small investment projects in the least developed countries. In recent years OPIC has also pioneered new ideas for encouraging investment in the LDCs. One such project is the First Philippine Capital Fund, a scheme to promote debt to equity swaps in the Philippines. The Fund, set up by a prominent U.S. investment banking firm, is to be capitalized by Philippines sovereign debt which is to be converted into local currency and invested in Philippine companies, especially government-owned firms being privatized. OPIC is providing up to $75 million in political risk and inconvertibility coverage for the Fund's investments. Debt-equity swaps are certainly not a panacea for LDC debt problems but can provide limited benefit especially if combined with privatization of state-owned enterprises.

Another new OPIC initiative is the Africa Growth Fund—an investment company to provide equity financing for American and local private sector investment in sub-Saharan Africa. In this case, OPIC is guaranteeing the $20 million in the investment company's notes.

In the area of investment promotion, OPIC mounts investment missions to selected LDCs. Usually carefully planned, OPIC investment missions have frequently produced tangible results. In a few cases, however, they have been organized primarily for political reasons as evidence of U.S. concern for a particular country and have resulted in little follow-on investment.

OPIC formerly also funded feasibility studies for investments and maintained an investment opportunity bank providing leads on projects in LDCs. Although OPIC does not rely on appropriated funds for its operations, it has had to discontinue these activities at the request of the Office of Management and Budget. This seems rather strange since the U.S. paid $150,000 in appropriated funds in 1987 for similar services to the Washington, D.C. office of the Investment Promotion Service (IPS) of the United Nations Industrial Development Organization (UNIDO).

The Washington IPS, one of nine such centers,[1] provides developed country companies with information on: LDC investment opportunities; LDC development plans, investment laws and incentives; and sources of project financing. In turn, the IPSs offer LDCs information on U.S. companies seeking investments overseas and resources for technology transfer. They also recruit business participants for promotional meetings in LDCs called "Investor Forums." In 1986, UNIDO's investment program worldwide successfully promoted 64 projects with a total of $265 million.[2] It is too soon, however, to judge the effectiveness of the U.S. office which only moved to Washington from New York in 1987.

Yet another organization working to overcome the economic obstacles to investment in developing countries is the International Finance Corporation (IFC). The IFC promotes economic growth in developing member countries by providing loans and equity to locally-owned companies or joint ventures with foreign investors. The IFC acts as a catalyst in structuring financial packages as well as providing its own funds. A new IFC instrument to encourage investment flows is known as the Guaranteed Recovery of Investment Principal (GRIP). Under this arrangement an investor deposits funds with the IFC in exchange for a long-term IFC note. The IFC then makes an investment in the LDC in its own name and assumes full risk of loss of principal for any reason. In return the IFC receives a negotiated front-end fee and a share of the profits. At the end of the agreed period, the investor may either acquire the shares or disengage and recover the principal amount invested from the IFC.[3]

Trade and tax benefits have also been used by developed countries to increase the expected return on investments in LDCs. Tax-sparing occurs when a developed country agrees to forego taxation of profits of its investors which are exempted from tax by developing countries as an investment incentive. The United States has always eschewed such agreements as being contrary to our overall tax policy. In the current budget and political climate in the United States, the opposition to tax

---

[1] The others are in Vienna, Austria; Paris, France; Cologne, Federal Republic of Germany; Milan, Italy; Tokyo, Japan; Seoul, South Korea; Warsaw, Poland; and Zurich, Switzerland.

[2] United Nations Industrial Development Organization, *What is UNIDO?* (Vienna, Austria: UNIDO, 1987).

[3] International Finance Corporation, *GRIP: Guaranteed Recovery of Investment Principal* (Washington, D.C.: IFC, 1986).

sparing is likely to remain strong. A number of other developed countries, however, have concluded tax sparing agreements.

U.S. trade preferences to LDCs under the U.S.-Caribbean Basin-Initiative (CBI) and the Generalized System of Preferences (GSP) may serve to encourage foreign investment. The duty free or other preferential treatment accorded to LDC exports by such programs can encourage foreign investors to produce in those countries as a means of getting around the barriers that would otherwise apply. For example, American investors appear to have been responsible for a good part of the growth in Singapore's GSP benefits from $300 million equal to 13 percent of total Singapore exports to the United States in 1980 to $1.3 billion equivalent to 33 percent of total Singapore exports to the United States in 1987.[1] The stock of U.S. direct investment in Singapore increased from $1.2 billion at yearend 1980 to $2.3 billion at yearend 1986.[2] The government of Singapore has estimated that 52 percent of its 1986 total worldwide exports came from subsidiaries of American firms operating there. While Singapore has been an attractive site for foreign investment for many reasons, the availability of GSP benefits has certainly been a factor. Because of its economic success, Singapore is to be graduated from the GSP program effective January 1, 1989.

On the other hand, the trade benefits granted to 28 Latin American countries under the CBI do not seem at least to date to be associated with an increase in U.S. direct investment in that region as a whole. Indeed, the U.S. direct investment position in the CBI countries fell from $13.6 billion at the end of 1984, the year CBI benefits became effective, to $13.4 billion at yearend 1986. The CBI countries' share of total U.S. direct investment abroad fell from 5.7 percent to 4.9 percent over the same period.[3]

The United States has also sought to use the level of GSP benefits as leverage in obtaining policy reforms in beneficiary countries. Some of these reforms can have a positive effect on the investment climate such as improved protection for intellectual property rights.

Since the U.S. GSP and similar programs of other developed countries are departures from the principal of most-favored-nation

---

[1]Office of the U.S. Trade Representative (USTR), *U.S. Imports of GSP Articles,* January-December 1980 and January-December 1987.

[2]U.S. Department of Commerce, *Survey of Current Business,* August 1982, p. 21 and August 1987, p. 65.

[3]Data supplied by U.S. Department of Commerce, International Trade Administration, Office of Trade and Investment Analysis.

(MFN) treatment, they can distort trade patterns and encourage the formation of trading blocs. There is some question, therefore, as to the desirability of extending such national programs rather than working for the multilateral reciprocal elimination of trade barriers under the General Agreement on Tariffs and Trade. The provision of the GATT allowing for "special and differential" treatment of LDCs does, however, permit LDCs to escape immediate GATT disciplines in some areas and this may encourage foreign investment.

A final U.S. government economic policy that works to encourage direct investment in developing countries is the 806/807 provision of the U.S. tariff code. This provision allows goods with at least a specified level of U.S. content to be re-imported duty free after having been previously exported for repair, processing and/or assembly abroad. In theory, the 806/807 provision applies to imports from all countries and thus does not require a GATT exception. In practice, however, it is used by U.S. firms almost exclusively to move labor-intensive production operations to developing countries in an effort to maintain the international competitiveness of, and some U.S. content in, the final product.[1]

Overcoming Political Obstacles

The political obstacles discussed above can be lumped into two general categories: those largely beyond and those within the control of the host government. In the former category one could place war, insurgency and severe political instability. Government policies would predominate in the other. Developed country governments and international organizations have attempted to neutralize the first category of political obstacles by providing insurance to cover non-commercial risks. That is the rationale for OPIC and the new Multilateral Investment Guarantee Agency (MIGA). OPIC insures U.S. companies against war, business interruption, expropriation, and currency inconvertibility. While expropriation and currency inconvertibility can be thought of as belonging more to the second category of political obstacle, they are frequently associated with political instability.

---

[1]Eric D. Ramstetter and Michael G. Plummer, "United States Direct Foreign Investment in ASEAN: A U.S. Perspective," pp. 33-34 (unpublished paper to be included in a forthcoming study of U.S.-ASEAN economic relations being coordinated by the East-West Center, Honolulu, Hawaii).

OPIC has, however, also played a positive role in overcoming the second category of political obstacles by encouraging LDC policy reform. One way OPIC does this is by not insuring projects that are subject to performance requirements which would likely reduce the expected trade benefits to the United States by 50 percent or more. In cases where the estimated benefits would be reduced by 25 to 49 percent, the OPIC Board will only approve projects in which there are exceptional circumstances which mitigate the presence of the performance requirements.

A number of LDC governments interested in improving their investment climates have consulted with OPIC about policy reforms that would help to attract investment. In particular, several Latin American countries, which have been liberalizing their investment rules, have been willing to conclude OPIC agreements but not full bilateral investment treaties (BITs). OPIC agreements, being largely procedural, are less sensitive politically than full BITs which create reciprocal international legal obligations concerning the treatment of investors.

OPIC's business-like operations and the fact that it does not rely on appropriated funds to cover its current operational expenditures have prompted several proposals over the past 15 years to turn its operations over to the private sector. In each instance it was determined that the private sector would not, in fact, be able to provide the coverages that OPIC does, especially in the areas of land-based war risk, inconvertibility risk and long-term expropriation coverage. The full faith and credit of the U.S. government behind OPIC and its ability to dispose of inconvertible local currencies by way of U.S. overseas mission expenses are factors that allow OPIC to operate where private insurers fear to tread. The amount of additional investment in LDCs due to the availability of OPIC insurance and financing is difficult to determine, yet there is a general consensus that OPIC programs are an effective way of encouraging the flow of capital and technology to the Third World.

The proposal for a Multilateral Investment Guaranty Agency (MIGA) was launched at the Seoul, Korea meetings of the World Bank and International Monetary Fund in 1985, although unsuccessful plans for similar bodies go back a number of years. Basically a multilateral OPIC, MIGA will have the primary function of insuring foreign investors in developing countries against political risks. At the urging of the United States and other developed countries, MIGA's Charter contains an explicit mandate of encouraging economic policy reform in recipient countries. The United States ratified the MIGA Charter in April 1988, and this latest member agency of the World Bank group should be operational by mid-1988. Theodore Moran has estimated that even under optimistic assumptions the additional investment likely to take place because of the availability of MIGA insurance is likely to be quite modest—perhaps no more than $200 million.[1] Even if Moran is correct, his estimate does not take into account the hoped-for beneficial effect on host government investment policies.

The President's 1983 investment policy statement mentioned above noted that the widespread international debt problems created a need for increased foreign investment and called on the World Bank and other multilateral development banks (MDBs) to explore ways of facilitating financial flows to the developing world. This call became more explicit in Treasury Secretary James Baker's debt strategy speech to the 1985 Bank/Fund meeting referred to above. One of the three legs of the Baker debt strategy has been policy reform by LDCs—policy reform that will reduce the obstacles to inflows of private capital. The MDBs are to assist this process by emphasizing more program (budget support) rather than traditional project lending and by making that lending conditional on the implementation of reforms by the recipient government.

Moran also sees other ways in which the World Bank could help in increasing foreign investment in the LDCs. These include making greater use in World Bank loan agreements of host country commitments not to change the fundamental laws or conditions affecting a large foreign investment project; expanding co-financing "B" loans to direct investment projects; and consideration of parallel World Bank loans to a government and a private investor for the same project. Under the last-mentioned technique, the loan to the private party would have a "political force majeure" clause, in effect guaranteeing the investors against political non-performance by the government party.[2]

The United States government encourages the World Bank to make increasing use of Moran's first suggestion but has reservations concerning the other two. The U.S. government fears that in many cases "B" loans,

---

[1]Theodore H. Moran, "The Future of Foreign Direct Investment in the Third World," in *Investing in Development: New Roles for Private Capital?*, Theodore H. Moran and contributors (New Brunswick, N.J.: Transaction Books, 1986), p. 13.

[2]Moran, pp. 13-14.

with their World Bank guarantee, would crowd out normal private sector lending. Thus, the U.S. government only supports "B" loans when they provide additionality—a difficult judgment call. The problem with parallel lending is that the political force majeure clauses could expose the Bank to losses which might injure its credit rating in world capital markets. Such parallel lending to the private sector would better be left to the International Finance Corporation, in the view of the U.S. government.

In addition to the financing programs discussed above, the International Finance Corporation has also started a Foreign Investment Advisory Service (FIAS). Not a promotion agency like UNIDO's IPS, FIAS helps interested member governments, generally LDCs, "to review and adjust policies, regulations and investment promotion strategies that affect foreign investment."[1] While FIAS frequently recommends that governments adopt the types of policy reforms discussed here, the fact that its services must be requested and generally paid for at least in part by the developing country, rather than being imposed, may make its advice more palatable. The policy role foreseen for MIGA raises the question of whether or not the FIAS operation should be transferred to that organization. Wherever the Service is located, it would seem to make sense to have a single organization serve all member agencies of the World Bank group.

While the programs discussed above offer the "carrots" of lending and insurance programs, the U.S. government also encourages LDCs to adopt sound investment policies, by threatening economic sanctions. Probably the best known is the Hickenlooper Amendment to the Foreign Assistance Act[2] which calls for cutting off economic assistance to countries whose governments expropriate American investors without the payment of prompt, adequate and effective compensation. The United States holds that this is the standard required under international law. Similar legislation governs U.S. government voting on loans to expropriating governments by multilateral development banks (the Gonzales Amendment) and the granting of duty-free tariff treatment to LDCs under the U.S. Generalized System of Preferences

---

[1] International Finance Corporation, *Foreign Investment Advisory Service* (Washington, D.C.: IFC, n.d.), p. 2.

[2] Section 620 (e) of the Foreign Assistance Act of 1961, as amended contained in *Legislation on Foreign Relations Through 1987* (Washington, D.C.: U.S. Government Printing Office, 1988), Vol. I, pp. 186-188.

(GSP). These "clubs" have rarely been wielded except in the case of a general deterioration of bilateral relations.

Although widely criticized by LDC governments, the sanctions may have had some deterrent effect on their actions and thereby contributed to the maintenance of, or return to, an environment conducive to foreign investment. For example, the expropriation sanctions were invoked against Ethiopia in 1979 after that government expropriated the property of all American investors without compensation. In 1987, however, Ethiopia settled all outstanding expropriation claims even though that Marxist regime remained ineligible for most types of assistance under other provisions of law. Evidently Ethiopia, which is again expressing interest in attracting foreign investment, felt it was worthwhile to settle the claims and have the Hickenlooper and related sanctions lifted.

Bilateral investment treaties (BITs) are international legal instruments under which each party reciprocally agrees to accord investments of the other party certain rights and to refrain from imposing a number of the more common political obstacles to foreign investment. These treaties are generally between a developed, capital exporting country and a developing, capital importing country. While the major European countries have been concluding BITs for a number of years, in some cases since the 1960s, the United States signed its first BIT only in 1982.

The United States sees BITs as achieving stability, predictability and transparency in host government policies affecting foreign investment. Specifically, a BIT does this by obliging each party to:

— extend national and most favored nation (MFN) treatment (with limited exceptions) to investors of the other party;
— avoid (or seek to avoid) the imposition of performance requirements;
— recognize that expropriation of an investor of the other party must be carried out in conformity with international law, including the payment of prompt, adequate and effective compensation;
— allow investors of the other party freely to remit earnings and capital; and
— accept impartial means of settling disputes with investors of the other party, including recourse at the investor's option to

17

the World Bank's International Center for the Settlement of Investment Disputes (ICSID).

The BITs concluded by the United States are generally more comprehensive and demanding than those of many other countries. The U.S. government believes, however, that BITs that do not contain meaningful standards will not produce the desired result of facilitating investment. Since a government will not normally conclude a BIT until its laws and regulations are in conformity with the treaty's standards, a BIT is principally an international commitment to maintaining those standards.

The United States has signed 10 BITs,[1] all of which were sent to the Senate in 1987; however, the Senate's advice and consent to ratification of the treaties was delayed for more than a year. Ironically, it was the BIT's tough standards that were an important factor in delaying Senate action. Some senators expressed concern that the BITs did not allow the U.S. government sufficient flexibility to take action against the investments in the United States of the partner developing country, should relations deteriorate. Since two of the pending BITs were with Panama and Haiti, the problem was not a hypothetical one, although it should be noted that the overwhelming amount of investment protected by the BITs is U.S. investment in the partner LDC. The administration believes that the BITs do allow the partner governments sufficient latitude to take measures to protect their essential security interests; nevertheless, the administration did not press for Senate action on either the Panama or Haiti treaties. The other eight finally received Senate advice and consent in October 1988.

While the BITs (and modern treaties of friendship, commerce and navigation) provide a legal basis for the protection of foreign investment on a bilateral basis, the United States and other governments have been interested in examining the possibilities of concluding multilateral agreements on investment standards which would help to overcome the obstacles to foreign investment, not only in LDCs but on a truly global basis. For decades economists have talked

---

[1]The United States has signed BITs with Bangladesh, Cameroon, Egypt, Grenada, Haiti, Morocco, Panama, Senegal, Turkey and Zaire.

about a "GATT for investment,"[1] but such an organization is far from being realized.

Richard Caves has stated that:

the national policies consistent with maximum global welfare from MNEs' [multinational enterprises'] activities diverge from those that appear to maximize national welfare. This proposition holds if countries fail to recognize the interdependent effects of their policies, and there is no guarantee in the theory of bargaining and retaliation that recognition will bring consensus on policies that maximize joint (global) welfare.[2]

Caves goes on to say that the General Agreement on Tariffs and Trade (GATT) has been able to overcome this difficulty through coincident tariff reductions, the benefits of which are spread fairly evenly among participating nations.

Caves maintains that there

is no comparable balance condition for a country's interests as source and host of MNEs. Therefore, no globally efficient change in policy that is not neutral between source and host can claim to spread its benefits equitably without side payments being made.[3]

Caves does point out, however, that as more and more nations become both home and host countries for investment, the balance of benefits and thus the basis for agreement on international standards will gradually improve.[4]

While the immediate prospects for a "GATT for Investment" appear slim, the United States has succeeded in having trade-related investment measures (TRIMs) included on the agenda in the GATT Uruguay Round of Multilateral Trade Negotiations. The United States had hoped to have the full range of investment issues and obstacles on

---

[1] See, for example, Paul M. Goldberg and Charles P. Kindleberger, "Toward a GATT for Investment," 2 *Law and Policy in International Business* (Summer 1970), pp. 295-325.

[2] Richard E. Caves, *Multinational Enterprise and Economic Analysis* (New York: Cambridge University Press, 1982), p. 295.

[3] Caves, p. 297.

[4] Caves, p. 297.

the table, but in the end settled for those related to trade. The mandate for the Negotiating Group on TRIMs agreed to at the 1986 Punta del Este ministerial meeting that launched the Uruguay Round provided that:[1]

> Following an examination of the operation of GATT Articles related to the trade restrictive and distorting effects of investment measures, negotiations should elaborate, as appropriate, further provisions that may be necessary to avoid such adverse effects on trade.

TRIMs include both incentives and performance requirements such as mandatory levels of exports and local content. Their significance as an obstacle to investment has been debated with no general consensus as to their effects. Stephen Guisinger holds that incentives do have a substantial effect on investors' locational decisions, while performance requirements do not.[2] On the other hand, Trevor Farrell, an economist from Trinidad and Tobago, disputes Guisinger's findings that incentives are important in determining investment flows.[3]

Theodore Moran and Charles Pearson, in a study prepared for OPIC using U.S. Department of Commerce data, conclude that performance requirements have a minimal distorting effect on trade. They suggest that the United States would be well advised to broaden the discussion of TRIMs in the Uruguay Round to include the locational effects of incentives used by many developed countries as well as the trade distorting effects of performance requirements, used mostly by LDCs.[4]

The U.S. government believes that government investment policies can have significant dampening and distorting impact on world trade, with effects comparable to tariffs and other non-tariff barriers. The U.S. delegation to the Uruguay Round has developed a number of case studies showing the trade effects of TRIMs and presented them to the Negotiating Group on TRIMs in Geneva. At present these studies remain

---

[1]GATT press release. GATT/1396, September 25, 1986.

[2] Stephen Guisinger, "Host Country Policies to Attract and Control Foreign Investment," in *Investing in Development: New Roles for Private Capital*, pp. 157-172.

[3]Trevor Farrell, "Incentives and Foreign Investment Decisions: an Opposing View," *The CTC Reporter*, No. 20 (Autumn 1985), pp. 39, 41-42.

[4]Theodore H. Moran and Charles Pearson, *Trade Related Investment Performance Requirements*, an unpublished study prepared for the Overseas Private Investment Corporation, March 1987, pp. 3-4.

restricted and are not releasable to the public. The U.S. government would certainly be willing, as Moran suggests, to discuss in the Uruguay Round the investment effects of incentives as well as the trade effects. The LDCs, however, are reluctant to discuss incentives at all and seem bent on limiting the scope of the negotiations as much as possible. The U.S. government remains committed to seeking GATT discipline over the use of TRIMs, but progress in the negotiations is likely to be slow.

The Organization for Economic Cooperation and Development (OECD) is the international body that has done most to deal with the policy obstacles to investment. Through the Capital Movements Code, the voluntary Guidelines for Multinational Enterprises, the Declaration on National Treatment and Incentives and Disincentives to Investment, and Consultation Procedures, the OECD has a fairly comprehensive set of instruments to deal with investment issues. The limitation of OECD membership to the industrial democracies, however, has kept it from being a major factor in U.S. efforts to reduce investment obstacles in the LDCs. Nevertheless, the OECD has recently begun to dialogue with LDCs on investment issues. An initial effort by the OECD Committee on International Investment and Multilateral Enterprises (CIME) was a four-day Roundtable on Investment held in Berlin in May 1986 with representatives from a number of developing countries. A major theme of the conference, which was co-sponsored by the OECD and the German Foundation for International Development (Deutsche Stiftung fuer internazionale Entwicklung), was the home and host country determinants of investment, in other words, government investment policies.

The OECD decided to follow up with a second roundtable in Tokyo in February 1989. This conference focused on the role foreign direct investment can play in the alleviation of LDC debt problems and in the transfer of emerging new technologies to the LDCs. The OECD Development Assistance Committee (DAC) has been examining internally how to strengthen the role of the private sector in development cooperation. In connection with this project, the DAC has been studying obstacles to foreign direct investment in developing countries.

The U.S. government strongly supports greater OECD involvement in investment issues with the LDCs. The organization's efforts might be more effective if the work of the various committees were somewhat better coordinated. Ideally, the responsibility for investment issues with the LDCs should be given to a single committee.

21

Since the United Nations is a near universal organization, one might think that it would be best placed to deal with the question of facilitating foreign investment flows to the LDCs. The United Nations Commission on Transnational Corporations, (The Commission), a subsidiary body of the Economic and Social Council (ECOSOC), was established in 1974 with the tasks of formulating and implementing a Code of Conduct on Transnational Corporations (TNCs), strengthening the ability of LDCs to deal with TNCs and developing an information system on these enterprises. The intergovernmental Commission is supported by the UN Centre on Transnational Corporations (the Centre), an arm of the UN Secretariat. The Centre is charged with carrying out the advisory and information gathering functions.

Unfortunately, in the view of the U.S. government, the work of these UN organizations to date on investment matters has been disappointing. Despite the changed, more positive attitude of LDCs and DCs alike toward foreign investment, the Commission continued to focus on TNC behavior as the main obstacle to beneficial foreign investment. Certainly, corporate behavior is relevant to the treatment accorded MNEs by governments. The decade-long negotiations on a Code of Conduct on TNCs have produced considerable agreement on standards for corporate conduct but remain deadlocked because of serious differences regarding the treatment of investment by governments.

Many LDCs and communist countries view the Code as closely tied to the New International Economic Order (NIEO) and the Charter of Economic Rights and Duties of States (CERDs), both of which were opposed by the United States and several other developed countries.[1] The U.S. government is not prepared to endorse a code that is inconsistent with the treatment provisions of U.S. bilateral investment treaties and U.S. government views on customary international law. The bloc politics of the UN system—which gives undue strength to the most hard line positions—has also hampered progress.

The U.S. government remains willing to support a UN Code that is voluntary, balanced to include rules on government treatment of

---

[1] Alan Keyes, "Prepared Statement of the Honorable Alan Keyes, Assistant Secretary of State for International Organization Affairs," contained in *Review of the U.N. Code of Conduct for Transnational Corporations*, Hearing before the Subcommittee on Human Rights and International Organizations of the Committee on Foreign Affairs, House of Representatives, Committee Print (Washington, D.C.: U.S. Government Printing Office, 1987) pp. 8-9.

investment as well as guidelines for enterprises, and one that is universally applicable to all MNCs, including those based in communist countries.[1] Nevertheless, given the lack of progress at the last three formal negotiating rounds and at an informal Roundtable on the Code held in Montreux, Switzerland in October 1986, the U.S. government believes that further formal negotiations on the Code should not be scheduled until there is clear evidence that the major outstanding issues can be resolved.[2] Even among the developing and communist countries, interest in the Code appears to be waning.

The U.S. government has also been unhappy about some of the work of the UN Centre on TNCs. In particular, the U.S. government found that the Centre's studies were critical of Western MNCs but largely ignored the investment activities of communist and LDC enterprises. The Centre's role in advising LDCs has also been of some concern to the United States to the extent that the Centre has played a role in actual negotiations between an LDC and an MNC. Recently, as a result of U.S. urging, the Centre has been given a more explicit mandate from the Commission, and it appears to be bringing greater balance into its work.

Conclusion

The discussion above has concentrated on LDC obstacles to increased foreign investment, but it needs to be noted that developed country economic policies can affect investment flows to the LDCs in a major way. Suitable macroeconomic policies by the OECD countries which encourage noninflationary growth and the eschewing of protectionism will help the market to direct capital and technology flows to the LDCs. If the United States and others do not keep their markets open to those products in which LDC exporters—including foreign-invested firms—have a comparative advantage, our advice to the LDCs about policy reform is likely to go unheeded. A first conclusion, then, is that the United States, as the world's largest market, has a particular responsibility to exercise leadership in this area.

A second conclusion is that the U.S. government should follow a basically neutral policy with regard to foreign investment. In the long run, this will help to avoid an inefficient allocation of resources and, in the case of an economic slowdown in the United States, charges that

---

1Keyes, p. 6.
2Keyes, p. 10.

the government is actively engaged in exporting jobs. With regard to investment in the LDCs, certain limited exceptions to this rule can be continued on development, market imperfection and infant industry grounds.

The first exception justifies our AID programs aimed at improving infrastructure, private sector development, etc. The second exception would allow OPIC and MIGA-type non-commercial risk insurance programs on the grounds that, by helping to neutralize political factors, investor decisions can bm made on strictly economic grounds. U.S. government support for investment missions, investment opportunity banks, and similar programs can be justified as helping to overcome the imperfect information that exists concerning investment possibilities in the developing world.

Finally, preferential tariff schemes which may encourage foreign investment, such as GSP and CBI, can be supported on grounds analogous to those supporting the concept of infant industry tariffs. The preferences should, however, be limited in duration to a reasonable period necessary for the LDC industries to become competitive. Following this argument, the recently announced graduation of Taiwan, South Korea, Hong Kong and Singapore from the GSP Program effective January 1, 1989, is certainly justified, given the evident competitiveness of many of their export industries.

As noted above, the U.S. government has active programs in all three categories of "exceptions" to a neutral investment policy. This writer would not advocate any new U.S. initiatives in this area and, indeed, suggest that it would be well to keep in mind the basic U.S. government preference for market solutions when implementing its current programs.

Since it does not appear feasible to negotiate a binding multilateral agreement dealing with investment policies in the foreseeable future, a third conclusion is that the U.S. government should continue to promote agreements that are limited, either in terms of scope or participation, wherever prospects for progress appear most likely. One vehicle is our bilateral investment treaty program.

Another promising area, where the United States is exercising leadership, is the GATT Uruguay Round negotiations on trade-related investment measures. It will be important, for the success of those negotiations, for the U.S. government to be able to demonstrate to the LDCs the benefits that they would derive from GATT discipline over TRIMs, including incentives. An offer of developed country willingness to limit the use of investment incentives, together with LDC as well as developed country willingness to curb the use of trade-distorting performance requirements, might provide one promising avenue of approach.

What attitude should the U.S. government take toward negotiations on non-binding codes of conduct as a means of overcoming the obstacles to investment in the LDCs? In a recent monograph, John Kline makes a forceful case for continuing to press for international regulation of investment via the code or "soft law" approach despite the current absence of pressure. Kline argues that:[1]

— The current eagerness of the developing world to attract foreign investment could easily fade and the more hostile LDC attitudes of the 1960s and early 1970s toward MNEs could return again;
— international business and pro-business governments may find that the "soft law" approach of codes may be preferable to other forms of regulation and could serve to restrain nationalistic actions; and
— an internationally agreed floor of responsibilities and practices for MNEs is needed to protect the interests of the least powerful.

On the other hand, codes have several serious shortcomings:

— Compromise on basic policy principles—such as the standards of international law—in order to reach agreement on a code could work against U.S. interests in other fora such as BIT negotiations or expropriation cases before ICSID;
— vague, essentially political codes may work to increase rather than decrease uncertainty, and actually discourage investment; and
— codes are difficult to apply in practice.

Some explanation is needed on the last point. Since codes are voluntary, attempts to implement them tend either to be trivial (MNEs should obey the laws of the countries in which they operate) or an

---

[1]John M. Kline, *Advantages of International Regulation: The Case for a Flexible, Pluralistic Framework* (unpublished monograph for the Lehrman Institute, International Regulation Series), November 13, 1986, pp. 33-35.

effort to create standards above and beyond national law. In the latter case, a host government may seek to impose discriminatory standards on MNCs, or a home country government be asked to impose its own standards extraterritorially. Codes tend to work best when the participating countries share common views on a wide variety of political, economic and social questions, as is generally the case among the OECD countries. Even within the OECD, however, considerable differences of opinion have arisen concerning the implementation of the organization's Guidelines for Multinational Enterprises. Some feel that governments should make judgments whether or not specific instances of corporate conduct violate the provisions of the Guidelines; others, including the United States, believe that neither the OECD nor its member countries should make such judgments.

While the U.S. government should maintain its willingness to consider non-binding codes of conduct, it should not, in view of the problems mentioned above, give them a high priority in terms of our efforts to overcome obstacles to investment in the LDCs.

Rather than emphasize codes, this writer, as a final conclusion, would concentrate a greater effort on policy dialogue between governments, and between governments and international organizations. Dialogue on investment issues can take place under a variety of forms including:

— a formal agreement (U.S.-Mexican Framework Agreement on Trade and Investment);
— informal but regular arrangements (ASEAN-U.S. Economic Dialogue);
— ad hoc meetings (OECD Roundtables with LDCs on investment issues); and
— meetings between LDCs and national or international financial organizations with policy reform mandates (MIGA, World Bank and regional MDBs, OPIC).

To the extent possible, private sector involvement is desirable and can help keep the governments focused on practical problems. As dialogue proceeds and consensus builds, the conclusion of binding undertakings may become possible either globally on a particular issue or on a number of issues among a few countries. Certainly this is the hope of the United States concerning trade-related investment measures in the Uruguay Round.

Dialogue, of course, implies a genuine willingness to listen to the other side's point of view as well as expressing one's own and to seek solutions to problems acceptable to all parties. As the Pontifical Commission "Iustitia et Pax" concluded with regard to the international debt crisis, international dialogue on removing obstacles to foreign investment in the LDCs will require:

> all people of good will to broaden their conscience to include these new, urgent and complex responsibilities, and to mobilize the full range of their possibilities for action in order to identify and implement solutions of solidarity.[1]

[1]Pontifical Commission "Iustitia et Pax," *At the Service of the Human Community: An Ethical Approach to the International Debt Question* (Vatican City: Polyglot Press, 1986), p. 31.

II. DO TRIPS TRIP UP FOREIGN INVESTMENT? AN INTERNATIONAL BUSINESS DIPLOMACY PERSPECTIVE*

By Theodore H. Moran and Charles S. Pearson

Introduction

Foreign direct investment is being hailed as a vehicle for accelerating economic development and ameliorating the commercial bank debt problem of developing countries. This chapter examines whether trade related investment performance (TRIP) requirements are a significant obstacle to increased foreign direct investment (FDI). The first section shows that despite a strong case for increased FDI, it is faltering. Section 2 defines TRIPs and explains why they are used. Section 3 presents empirical data on the form, country and sector incidence of TRIP requirements, and examines their economic effects with a view toward understanding whether they are a significant obstacle to foreign direct investment. Section 4 examines U.S. policy toward TRIP requirements, and the final section presents conclusions.

---

* This is a revised version of an article which originally appeared as "Tread Carefully in the Field of Trip Measurements," in the March 1988 number of The World Economy, the quarterly journal of the Trade Policy Research Centre, London, and draws on research contained in a previous work by the same authors, *Trade Related Investment Performance Requirements*, a study prepared for the Overseas Private Investment Corporation, March 1987.

28

Background

Foreign Direct Investment

The argument for increased foreign direct investment in developing countries is timely and compelling. At its best, FDI brings capital, technology and international marketing and management skills to countries where these resources are in short supply. Foreign direct investment harmonizes nicely with current efforts to promote private sector initiatives, and resonates sympathetically with the call for privatization of parastatal enterprise.

The rehabilitation of foreign direct investment as a vehicle for development is in part a result of increasing sophistication by developing countries. They have gained experience in negotiations with foreign investors and have come to realize that within limits, and by adroit policy, they can share in the surplus from FDI. The principal channels for distributing the surplus between investor and host government—and hence the principal arena for contention—are tax, employment and trade practices. International investors, mainly multinational enterprises, have themselves gained considerable experience and have shown remarkable adaptability to host government requirements concerning the full array of investment conditions— ownership arrangements, profit repatriation practices, employment, environmental restrictions, and so forth. Consistently, MNCs have insisted that it is the predictability and stability of host country policies and performance requirements, and not their absolute level, that determines the investment decision.

Increasing sophistication, confidence, and experience by host governments and MNCs is half the story in explaining the improved relationship between foreign investors and Third World countries. The other half has its origins in the debt crisis. Many (not all) developing countries desperately need foreign exchange, export marketing channels, and relief from servicing foreign debt. Foreign direct investment, through debt-equity swaps but more importantly through increased traditional investment vehicles, is attractive because it can provide new capital, improve export earnings, and convert fixed foreign exchange obligations (debt service) to external payment, conditional on the FDI actually earning a profit. The debt crisis has forced a new realism on developing countries, and in the recent congenial atmosphere

29

of privatization, deregulation and structural adjustment, the virtues of FDI appear to shine more clearly.

Given the newly enthusiastic view on foreign direct investment, the performance, at least by the United States, is disappointing. Table 1 shows that the U.S. direct investment position in manufacturing and petroleum in developing countries has been virtually stagnant since 1982, with the cumulative net inflow valued at only $2.5 billion. The reinvestment ratio in petroleum has become negative and reinvested earnings in manufacturing amounted to only $702 million in 1986.

Some of this disappointing performance must be the result of the debt crisis itself. A considerable portion of FDI is for the purpose of serving host country markets, and with demand in these countries flat or declining, the incentive for investment is undercut. As illustration, U.S. foreign direct investment in petroleum and manufacturing in heavily indebted Latin America rose by only $625 million from year end 1985 to year end 1986. Nevertheless, it is conceivable that onerous investment performance requirements have also worked against the flow of FDI, and it is to this question we now turn.

TRIPs Defined and Explained

Trade related investment performance requirements may be defined as host government policies designed to encourage local purchase of inputs by foreign-owned firms, and policies to encourage these firms to export. The definition is arbitrary but is formulated to include the most central policies—local content requirements and export minima—and exclude more general policies that do not distinguish between domestic and foreign-owned firms, such as high tariffs on imported inputs or export subsidy schemes available regardless of the firm's ownership. The definition is also broad enough to include not only numerical domestic content and export minima requirements, but conditional packages of incentives and disincentives that lead or push firms to increase local purchase of inputs, and that direct production toward exports, in order to gain access to the incentives or to avoid the penalties. The definition also excludes a number of investment performance requirements that may have an indirect trade effect, but which are motivated by non-trade concerns (e.g., employment, profit repatriation, environmental standards). Within this definition it is sometimes useful to distinguish (1) between TRIP requirements that set numerical standards for import content or export minima and those that

30

do not; (2) between TRIP requirements that offer conditional benefits to the foreign investor and those that are mandatory and offer no quid pro quo to the investor and (3) between TRIP requirements that relate export performance to import performance (i.e., "balancing" requirements) and those that do not.

TRIP requirements by themselves should be viewed as disincentives to investment. Local content requirements, if binding (i.e., they actually motivate the investor to change his buying or selling arrangements) may increase costs, decrease earnings and, ceterius paribus, make the firm's foreign investment less competitive. Export minima, if binding, may require intra-firm subvention of exports, decrease earnings, and make the foreign investment less attractive.

This raises two questions. First, why do firms go along with TRIP requirements? Second, why do host countries, which presumably want FDI, establish TRIP requirements in the first place? The first question is in effect answered in the empirical section. Host countries frequently offer some form of quid pro quo to offset the additional burden of TRIP requirements—preferential tax status, access to foreign exchange, import protection, a quasi-monopoly or other such benefits. Thus MNCs tend to be compensated for whatever additional costs are incurred by TRIP requirements. This is not to say the "package" is efficient, but it does help explain why MNCs have not led the fight against TRIPs requirements. By and large, they get a cozy deal, with additional costs more than offset by monopoly status, favorable tax treatment or some other form of host government largess. The widespread existence of favorable quid pro quo type policies by host governments is the single most important reason for believing that TRIP requirements are not a major impediment for FDI.

Why do host countries participate in this charade, taking from the MNC with one hand and returning favors with the other? There are several explanations. First, as a practical matter TRIP requirements represent an explicit commitment to increasing the supply of or conserving foreign exchange. This commitment is useful in "selling" a particular foreign investment to the populace—a tangible benefit that can be paraded—and in reassuring government officials that the foreign exchange consequences of the investment decisions are known and positive. Economists are fond of pointing out that foreign exchange earned from exports or saved through import substitution is properly considered the end result of appropriate macro-economic policies, especially exchange rate policy. But government officials in debt-ridden economies subject to acute foreign exchange scarcity are apt to dispense with these niceties and focus on the direct foreign exchange consequences of particular investment decisions. This is unfortunate, as theory suggests that the increased costs accompanying TRIP requirements may actually decrease the international competitive position of the TRIP imposing country, and can exacerbate foreign exchange scarcity.[1]

A second reason, not altogether unjustified, is that TRIP requirements can correct certain market distortions. For example, MNCs may be insensitive to international comparative advantage in their production-location and trade decisions, and reluctant to disturb intra-corporate, international trade patterns. TRIP requirements can overcome an anti-export, pro-import bias of MNCs.[2] This bias arises from the firm's desire not to disturb its existing production and marketing arrangements. Also, MNCs make investment decisions under conditions of great uncertainty and without full exploration of alternative production location choices. Given this uncer l ainty, and recognizing that investment often is in oligopolistic industries that offer some choice of investment location, TRIP requirements may force production location decisions on firms, accelerating infant industry development. Moreover TRIP requirements may be purely defensive on the part of some host authorities. For example, a firm doing business in one country may be lured into producing inputs in another country by a variety of incentives. The first country may counter this lure by establishing a domestic content law, forcing the firm to return to the local source of inputs.

Also, the availability of a diverse set of incentives and disincentives provides flexibility in negotiating with potential investors—additional chips. This may allow a bargain in which an incentive with high value to the investor and low marginal cost to the host country, say access to an existing free trade zone, are traded for a

---

[1] Gene Grossman, "The Theory of Domestic Content Protection and Content Preference," *Quarterly Journal of Economics* 96 (November 1981), p. 583-604; Carl Davidson, Steven J. Matusz, Mordechai E. Kreinin, "Analysis of Performance Standards for Foreign Investment" (November 1985), *18 Canadian Journal of Economics*, p. 876-890.

[2] G. K. Helleiner, "Manufactured Exports from Less-Developed Countries and Multinational Firms," *Economic Journal* 83 (1973); Rhys Jenkins, "The Export Performance of Multinational Corporations in Mexican Industry," *Journal of Development Studies* 15 (1979).

performance requirement of low marginal cost to the investor but high real or perceived value to the host country, say an explicit commitment for local R&D expenditure. Also, when the incentives and restrictions (disincentives) are negotiated for specific investments, an extensive and flexible set of incentive and disincentive measures can be used to exploit the firm-specific desire to invest, with the host government acting somewhat in the manner of a discriminating monopolist. Finally, performance requirements and other disincentives may be imposed after the investment has occurred, essentially changing the terms of the investment bargain after resources have been committed.[1]

Understanding the motivations for TRIP requirements does not make them economically rational. By and large, there are more efficient policies for these objectives. The economic costs of TRIP requirements frequently go unrecognized. As disincentives to investment they increase cost to the firm and, for domestic content type requirements, tend to decrease production, employment, value added, and exports of the downstream industry, unless matched by distortive policies that favor the downstream industry, such as granting the downstream firm a monopoly position in the domestic market. By themselves, domestic content type TRIP requirements reduce or make negative the effective rate of protection in the downstream industry. Export minima also create distortions. When they are linked to a set of incentives such as a monopoly position in the home market they become, in effect, state-induced intra-firm subsidies to export. The situation then resembles international dumping, abetted by host government policy.

Empirical Evidence

Whether or not TRIP requirements constitute a significant barrier to FDI depends on their extent and characteristics. No comprehensive current inventory of TRIP requirements exists, but there is scattered evidence of varying quality, reviewed here. There are several reasons for the indifferent quality of the data. These include inconsistent definitions, no data collection effort at the international level, and the fact that many TRIP requirements are specific to a particular sector or even a particular project. Moreover, many are conditional and may not

---

[1]For the idea of the "obsolescing bargain," see Raymond Vernon, *Sovereignty at Bay: The Multinational Spread of U.S. Enterprises* (New York: Basic Books, 1971); Theodore H. Moran, ed., *Multinational Corporations: The Political Economy of Foreign Direct Investment* (Lexington, Mass.: D.C. Heath, 1985).

be triggered in practice, may not be enforced, or may be renegotiated by the firm on a case by case basis. Finally, there is little incentive for disclosure by either the host government or the firm that has negotiated a sweet deal.

U.S. Department of Commerce Benchmark Survey (1977 and 1982) and USTR Update

The Bureau of Economic Analysis, U.S. Department of Commerce, surveyed investment performance requirements as part of its 1977 *Survey of U.S. Direct Investments Abroad*, and the results are summarized by Harvey Bale and David Walters.[1]

The principal finding with regard to the characteristics and extent of TRIP requirements are:

(a) As indicated in Table 2, only 2 percent of U.S. foreign affiliates in developed countries were subject to export requirements, 3 percent to maximum import requirements and 3 percent to local content requirements. The percentage for affiliates located in developing countries are higher but still low. The relatively low percentage surprised the USTR analysts, who surmised that the incidence of TRIP requirements may have risen since 1977. (But see point (e) below.)

(b) The sectoral breakdown of performance requirements of all types (including non-TRIP requirements) is presented in Table 3. Mining and transportation equipment (automobiles) are the most frequent sectors for performance requirements and together account for 8.5 percent of U.S. foreign direct investment. Downstream processing requirements in the mining sector can be thought of as a "downstream local content" or maximum export requirement. They are thus the converse of traditional TRIP requirements.

(c) The automotive sector appears especially subject to TRIP requirements. As shown in Table 4, the automotive sector combines both extensive use of local content and export requirements and high levels of protection. The U.S.-Canadian Auto Agreement has TRIP-like requirements in that it specifies for every car sold in Canada by U.S. firms, a car must be manufactured there for domestic sale or export.

(d) Of 17 "selected countries with significant occurrences" of local content and export requirements, 13 were LDCs and four were developed

---

[1]Harvey E. Bale, Jr., and David A. Walters, "Investment Policy Aspects of U.S. and Global Trade Interests," *Looking Ahead* (Washington, D.C.: U.S. International Trade Commission, 1982).

countries. Within these 17 countries, the U.S. foreign direct investment position as of 1981 was $26 billion in the 13 LDCs (28 percent of the total) and $68 billion (72 percent of the total) in the four developed countries.

(e) The 1982 Benchmark Survey has not been fully analyzed, but preliminary analysis shows that only 1.6 percent of U.S. affiliates are subject to minimum export requirements, 1.5 percent to maximum import levels and 1.0 percent to local content requirements. These data are not directly comparable to the 1977 survey as firms with sales under $3 million were excluded from the 1982 survey.

Study by the U.S. International Trade Commission on the Impact of Foreign Trade-Related Performance Requirements on U.S. Industry and Foreign Investment Abroad

In 1982 Ambassador Brock, the U.S. Trade Representative, requested that the ITC prepare a substantive quantitative review of the economic impact of foreign performance requirements on U.S. trade; on U.S. production and employment; and on foreign investment patterns and income for three industries characterized by significant foreign investment. Those industries were motor vehicles, chemicals (including pharmaceuticals), and high-technology goods. The coverage of the study represented 70 percent of total U.S. direct investment abroad in motor vehicles and equipment and 90 percent of total U.S. direct investment abroad in office, computing and accounting machines in 1981. According to the ITC, the report contained confidential business information and was never released to the public. From talking with individuals familiar with the report, it is possible to summarize many of the results without compromising business confidentiality.

The report defined "performance requirements" as import maxima (aimed at spurring domestic production), minimum export requirements, and local content rules. For the purpose of this study, the term TRIP requirements will be used. Among the principal findings with regard to the characteristics and extent of TRIP requirements are:

(a) In the chemical industry, 40 percent of the U.S. chemical producers having direct investment abroad reported having one or more affiliates operating under TRIP requirements (22 firms). Of the 367 affiliates producing chemicals and allied products, 45 affiliates (12 percent) ere operating under these TRIPs. Various import restrictions were most commonly reported (34 affiliates or 9 percent of all affiliates), followed by minimum export requirements (15 affiliates or 4 percent), and local content rules (10 affiliates or 3 percent).

(b) Although chemicals affiliates were reported to be subject to TRIP requirements around the world (17 countries), the TRIPs were most often used in developing countries (12 countries), particularly Latin America (6 countries), and in one developed country.

(c) More than 80 percent of the U.S. motor vehicle and motor vehicle equipment manufacturers having direct investment abroad reported having one or more foreign affiliates operating under TRIP requirements (17 firms out of a total of 21). Of the 131 affiliates producing motor vehicles and equipment, 54 affiliates (41 percent) were operating under TRIPs. Local content requirements were most frequently reported (49 affiliates or 37 percent of total affiliates), followed by import restrictions (40 affiliates or 31 percent) and export minimums (15 affiliates or 11 percent).

(d) Although motor-vehicle affiliates were reported to be subject to TRIP requirements throughout the world (17 countries), such requirements were most often used in developing countries (10 countries), particularly Latin America (7 countries), and two developed countries (Canada and Australia).

(e) Slightly more than one-third of the U.S. office, computing, and accounting machines equipment manufacturers having direct foreign investment reported having one or more foreign affiliates operating under TRIP requirements (6 firms out of 16). Of the 57 affiliates producing these products, 11 affiliates (19 percent) were operating under TRIPs. All of the parent firms had affiliates subject to export minimums (8 affiliates), most to import restrictions (8 affiliates of 5 firms), and half had affiliates with local content rules (6 affiliates).

(f) Very few countries were reported to be imposing performance requirements specifically directed at the office, computing and accounting machine industry. Survey respondents indicated that affiliates were subject to performance requirements in only three countries in 1981, Mexico, Brazil, and Spain.

The Study by Stephen Guisinger and Associates (1985)[1]

Stephen Guisinger and his associates, in research sponsored by the International Finance Corporation of the World Bank, surveyed by interview more than 30 firms (MNCs) concerning 74 investment decisions located in more than 20 developed and developing countries. Four sectors were covered: food processing, automobiles, computers, and petrochemicals. A principal purpose of the study was to determine the effectiveness of incentive and performance requirements in altering the investment and operational decisions of foreign investors.

The principal findings with regard to the characteristics and extent of TRIP requirements are:

(a) Thirty-eight of the 74 cases (51 percent) in the sample were subject to explicit TRIP requirements (and in some of the other cases the incentive package was tied to trade performance).

(b) Nine of the 12 cases (75 percent) in the automobile sector were subject to TRIP requirements. In contrast, TRIP requirements in the computer industry were infrequent and unimportant. In the food processing industry, 12 out of 25 firms (48 percent) were subject to TRIP requirements. With regard to the petrochemical industry, most of the TRIP requirements have been traditionally located in the developed countries that buy the products (Japan, Western Europe); the locus of TRIP requirements is shifting, however, to the LDC producer states.

(c) Explicit performance requirements (including TRIP requirements) were more frequent in developing than developed countries because of the greater frequency of a large protected international market, a condition supportive of performance requirements. "However," the authors concluded, "it bears repeating that developed countries achieve much the same result using implicit performance requirements."[2]

---

[1] Stephen E. Guisinger and Associates, *Investment Incentives and Performance Requirements* (New York, N.Y.: Praeger, 1985); see also, "Host Country Policies to Attract and Control Foreign Investment," in Theodore H. Moran and contributors, *Investing in Development: New Roles for Private Capital?* (Washington, D.C.: Overseas Development Council, 1986).

[2] *Investment Incentives and Performance Requirements*, op. cit., p. 320.

U.S.T.R. Computerized Inventory

The Office of the U.S. Trade Representative maintains a computerized inventory of foreign barriers to U.S. investment.[1] The current list covers 92 industrial, developing and centrally planned economies, and is presented by country, industry, type of barrier, law vs. policy, and a brief explanation. The inventory is of limited usefulness for our purposes, as it is not known how exhaustive it is (and thus how representative), how the policies and laws are implemented, and whether any U.S. investment is affected. In short, the inventory appears to be drawn from legal and regulatory documents and how they applied in any particular instance is unknown.

Despite these limits, Tables 5 and 6 try to distill some information regarding TRIP requirements.

(a) Table 5 shows that for the 92 countries a total of 498 investment barriers were identified. Of the 498 barriers 91, or 18 percent, were apparently trade related, and of these 59 appeared to be of the local content type and 33 of the export requirement type. (These data should be used very cautiously because sufficient information is not always available to clarify the barriers with certainty.) Good data on TRIP requirements by sector could not be distilled but the frequency of TRIP requirements in the automotive sector is apparent.

(b) Table 5 also classifies TRIP requirements by country groups. Industrial countries accounted for 23 percent of all countries inventoried and 19 percent of all TRIP requirements. Centrally planned economies, including China, accounted for 10 percent of countries inventoried and 3 percent of TRIP requirements. Developing countries accounted for 67 percent of countries inventoried and 77 percent of TRIP requirements. The percent of local content of total TRIP requirements was slightly higher in developing countries (66 percent) than in industrialized countries (59 percent), with export requirements being more frequent in industrialized countries.

(c) Table 6 attempts to identify TRIP requirements that establish specific numerical requirements for local content on export levels and those that appear negotiable or discretionary. Again, the information is not sufficient to be certain in many cases. It would appear, though, that about 40 percent set numerical targets and 60 percent are negotiable/discretionary. Specific numerical targets appear more

---

[1]Office of Investment Policy, USTR, "Inventory of Investment Barriers," 11/22/85.

frequent in developing countries (50 percent) and less frequent in industrialized countries (18 percent). Finally, specific numerical targets appear to be set in 47 percent of the local-content type TRIP requirements and in 33 percent of the export-type TRIP requirements.

(d) The Office of the United States Trade Representative is also required under Section 303 of the 1984 Trade Act to publish an annual report of significant foreign trade barriers and distortions to trade, including significant barriers affecting investment.[1] The 1986 report covers 40 countries accounting for 78 percent of all 1985 U.S. export. A quantitative description of investment barriers—including TRIP requirements—is presented, but no numerical estimates are made of the impact on U.S. trade.

OPIC

The Overseas Private Investment Corporation, an agency of the U.S. government, is required by law to examine TRIP requirements in determining whether a particular investment qualifies for OPIC insurance or funding. In performing this function, by 1986 they had undertaken TRIP investigations in approximately 642 projects. The general findings as to extent and characteristics have been summarized by OPIC staff and are reported in Table 7. The table indicates 40 percent of all OPIC projects are subject to some TRIP requirements, with the highest proportion in the Near East and the lowest in Africa.

In evaluating these results and comparing them to the Guisinger study, it should be remembered that the universe of OPIC projects is not congruent with the universe of U.S. foreign direct investment or the Guisinger sample. For example, OPIC does not insure projects in Mexico and Venezuela, both of which are said to use TRIP requirements extensively. OPIC is also required by another provision of the law to decline insurance for those projects which will have a substantial adverse affect on U.S. employment, so that entire industries such as the automotive industry are unlikely to become OPIC clients. By sector, minerals and energy were most likely to be subject to TRIP requirements and banking and finance least likely.

---

[1]Office of the United States Trade Representative, *1986 Report on Foreign Trade Barriers* (Washington, D.C.: GPO, 1986).

In an effort to refine these data, a sample of 50 OPIC projects were examined by the authors in greater detail to illustrate the nature of the TRIP requirements.[1]

OPIC's summary analysis of each project, identified by country and sector, was examined in light of eight questions:

(1) Are there any TRIP requirements that may affect this investment?

(2) If yes, do they appear to be local content, export or balancing of import and export type requirements?

(3) For local content type requirements, does the regulation suggest that ceterius paribus a preference be given for domestic inputs (e.g., when price, quality, terms are equal)?

(4) Do the TRIP requirements appear to be the result of general regulations or specific to this particular investment?

(5) Do the TRIP requirements set numerical targets (either percent or absolute)?

(6) Does the firm receive investment incentives or other favorable treatment in return for its trade performance?

(7) Are the TRIP requirements binding or redundant?

(8) What is the principal reason for OPIC's determination?

The results of this research are reported in Table 8 and summarized in Table 9. The results are only preliminary, as in some cases it was not possible to answer the question with certainty. The sample projects are concentrated in Central America and the Caribbean (40 percent) and Asia (24 percent) with the others distributed between Africa and the Middle East.

Forty-eight percent of the sample projects appeared to be subject to TRIP requirements, with some combination of export and import requirements most frequently used (50 percent of TRIP projects). A balancing of imports and exports was required in 29 percent of the projects subject to TRIP requirements. Of the 17 projects in which some import limit or local content requirement occurred, 10 appeared to imply that domestic products were to be used if available at comparable price, quality, etc. (ceterius paribus basis). One can argue that on its face this performance requirement is neither onerous nor distortive.

---

[1] *Trade Related Investment Performance Requirements*, loc. cit.

Only two of the projects appeared to be subject to TRIP requirements that were specific to the project and not the result of more general legislation, although this does not mean that the precise requirements were not tailored to the project in many of the other cases.

Twenty-nine percent of projects subject to TRIP requirements set numerical targets. In 63 percent of TRIP requirement cases, investors received some form of favorable treatment in return for compliance with TRIP requirements.

Other Sources of Information

Scattered evidence on TRIP requirements can be found in a number of other sources. Richard Robinson, in a research report for the International Chamber of Commerce,[1] lists seven general patterns of government policy toward foreign investment, ranging from unrestricted entry and the absence of regulations to virtual protection of foreign direct investments. In discussing examples of five types of requirements, the report provides some detail on incentives and performance requirements for the five countries (Hong Kong, Ireland, Egypt, the Philippines, and Yugoslavia).

The Labor-Industry Coalition for International Trade (LICIT) published in 1981 a study of performance requirements that includes listings, by country, of local content and minimum export requirements, along with analysis and discussion of policy options.[2]

Finally, the IMF, drawing in part from its Annual Report on Exchange Arrangements and Exchange Restrictions, has compiled a list of restrictions and regulations concerning foreign investment among 25 major developing country borrowers. Information on TRIP requirements, however, is very sketchy.

---

[1] Richard D. Robinson, *Foreign Investments in the Third World: A Comparative Study of Selected Developing Country Investment Promotion Programs.* (Washington, D.C.: U.S. Chamber of Commerce, 1980).

[2] Labor-Industry Coalition for International Trade, *Performance Requirements* (Washington, D.C.: LICIT, 1981).

Table 1
U.S. Foreign Direct Investment

	Direct Investment Position Developing Countries Manufacturing and Petroleum (a) (billion $)	Reinvestment Ratio: Manufacturing	Petroleum (%)
1981	31.7	54.0	42.0
1982	35.3	17.0	24.0
1983	35.3	0	5.0
1984	36.9	55.0	28.0
1985	35.9	41.0	0
1986	37.8	30.0	0

Source: U.S. Department of Commerce, *Survey of Current Business,* various issues.
(a) "Other" foreign direct investment, excluded i this table, is m ·'·'y in bank and non-bank financial firms.

Table 2
Percent of U.S. Foreign Affiliates
Subject to Performance Requirements

	Developed Countries	Developing Countries (percent)	Total World
Affiliates Subject to:			
Minimum Export Requirements	2	1	3
Maximum Import Requirements	3	1	5
Minimum Local Content Requirements	3	1	6

Source: "The Use of Investment Incentives and Performance Requirement by Foreign Governments." Office of International Investment, International Trade Administration, U.S. Department of Commerce, October 1981.
Note: These percentages cannot be cumulated as one affiliate may be subject to multiple performance requirements.

Table 3

Performance Requirements by Industry (a)

Industry	% of U.S. Affiliates Subject to Performance Requirements	% Distribution of U.S. Direct Investment 1981
Total	14	100
Mining	27	3.3
Petroleum	16	22.9
Manufacturing	19	40.7
Food Products	21	4.0(b)
Chemicals	19	8.8
Primary & Fabricated Metals	18	2.9
Non-electrical Marketing	14	7.4
Electrical Marketing	21	3.3
Transportation Equipment	27	5.2
Other	17	9.1
Trade	9	12.4
Finance, Insurance, Real Estate	8	15.4
Other	10	5.3

Source: Harvey Bale and David Walters, "Investment Policy Aspects of U.S. and Global Trade Interests" Looking Ahead, National Planning Association, Vol. IX, No. 1, January 1986.
(a) Includes TRIP and non-TRIP requirements.
(b) Reported at 40.2%, an apparent misprint, no original.
Note that 58 percent of all affiliates subject to at least one performance requirement were subject to a non-TRIP type performance requirement.

Table 4
Local Content Requirements for Passenger Cars in Selected Countries as a Percentage of Final Value

	Required Local Content %	Ad Valoren Import Tariff %	1981 Production (000)	Export Requirement
Argentina	88	55	140	Yes
Australia	85	35-58	343	Yes
Brazil	95	182-205	621	Yes
Chile	30	20-60	21	No
Colombia	33	180	36	Yes
Egypt	15-40	85-200	17	No
Greece	25	10-21	5	Yes
India	*	*	42	No
Malaysia	18	60-100	86	No
Mexico	50-75	100	355	Yes
Morocco	40-50	57-97	14	No
Nigeria	30-100	33-200	85	No
Peru	30	66	22	No
Philippines	63	30-100	25	Yes
Portugal	22	**	61	No
So.Africa	66	20-100	301	No
So.Korea	20-95	100-150	67	No
Spain	55	68	855	Yes
Taiwan	70	65-75	86	No
Thailand	35	150	27	No
Venezuela	53	120	83	Yes

*Import license for passenger car imports rarely issued. Companies are nationally owned and are encouraged to source nearly 100 percent of their inputs.
**Specific duty.
Source: U.S. Department of Commerce; and reprinted from Bale and Walters, op.cit.

Table 5
TRIP Requirements by Type and Country Group

Country Group	Number of Countries	Number of Investment Barriers	Number of Countries Imposing TRIPs	TRIP Requirements Total	TRIP Requirements Local Content	TRIP Requirements Export Minimum
Total	92	498	40	90	57	33
Industrial	21		8	17	10	7
Developing	62		30	70	46	23
Latin America	18		12	29	20	9
Africa	26		7	9	7	2
Other	18		11	32	20	12
Centrally Planned Economies	9		2	3	1	2

Source: Derived from USTR "Inventory of Investment Barriers," 11/21/85.

Table 6
TRIP Characteristics

Country Groups	Total TRIP Requirements	Specific Numerical Targets Local Content	Specific Numerical Targets Export	Negotiable/ Discretionary
Total	90	27	11	52
Industrial	17	3	0	14
Developing	70	24	11	35
Latin America	29	10	5	14
Africa	9	3	0	6
Other	32	11	6	15
Centrally Planned Economies	3	0	0	3

Source: Derived from USTR "Inventory of Investment Barriers," 11/12/85.

Table 7
OPIC Experience with TRIP Requirements
(682 projects)

	TRIP Requirements (%)	No TRIP Requirements (%)
By Region:		
All Countries	40	60
Near East	50	50
East Asia	41	59
South Asia	41	59
Caribbean & Latin America	33	67
Africa	28	72
By Sector:		
All Sectors	40	60
Minerals & Energy	75	25
Manufacturing	45	55
Construction & Services	38	62
Agribusiness & Food	24	76
Banking & Finance	negligible	100

Table 8
OPIC Sample

Case No.	Region	Sector	1	2	3	4	5	6	7	8
1.	Africa	Lumber & Wood Products	Y	B	N	G	Ym	Y	NB	R
2.	Central America & Caribbean	Horticulture	Y	X	NA	G	N	Y	NB	NXUS
3.	Central America & Caribbean	Horticullture	N							
4.	Middle East	Chemicals	N							
5.	Asia	Electric Equipment	N							
6.	Middle East	Construction	N							
7.	Asia	Glass	Y	M,X,B	N	S	Yx	N	BIND	NUSXD
8.	Africa	Lumber & Wood Products	Y	M,X,B	N	G	N	Y	NB	R
9.	Asia	Chemicals	N							
10.	Central America & Caribbean	Hotels	N							
11.	Asia	Food Products	Y	X,M	?	S	Yx	N	NB	R
12.	Asia	Food Products	Y	M,B	Y	G	N	N	NB	NUSXD
13.	Central America & Caribbean	Agricultural Crops	Y	M,X	Y	G	N	Yx	NB	R
14.	Central America & Caribbean	Misc. Manufactures	N							
15.	Central America & Caribbean	Horticulture	Y	X	NA	G	N	Y	NB	R
16.	Central America & Caribbean	Agricultural Crops	Y	X	NA	G	N	Y	NB	R
17.	Africa	Electrical Equipment	N							
18.	Latin America	Hotels	Y	M	N	G	N	N	NB	R
19.	Africa	Chemicals	Y	M	?	G	N	N	NB	R
20.	Africa	Metal Mining	N							

47

Case No.	Region	Sector	1	2	3	4	5	6	7	8
21.	Central America & Caribbean	Metal Mining	N							
22.	Central America & Caribbean	Hotels	N							
23.	Central America & Caribbean	Hotels	N							
24.	Central America & Caribbean	Wholesale Trade	N							
25.	Middle East	Chemicals	N							
26.	Asia	Hotels	Y	M	Y	G	N	N	NB	R
27.	Latin America	Oil & Gas Extraction	Y	M	Y	G	N	N	NB	NUSXD
28	Central America & Caribbean	Hotels	N							
29.	Latin America	Wholesale Trade	Y	X	NA	G	N	Y	BIND	XUSD OUSM
30.	Africa	Electrical Equipment	N							
31.	Middle East	Fabricated Metal Prods.	N							
32.	Asia	Business Services	N							
33.	Central America & Caribbean	Apparel & Textiles	Y	X	NA	G	N	Y	NB	R
34.	Central America & Caribbean	Hotels	N							
35.	Asia	Chemicals	N							
36.	Asia	Food Products	Y	X,M,B	Y	G	N	Y	NB	R
37.	Central America & Caribbean	Fabricated Metal Prods	Y	X,M	Y	G	N	Y	NB	R
38.	Latin America	Banking	N							
39.	Central America & Caribbean	Electrical Equipment	Y	X	NA	G	N	Y	NB	R
40.	Central America & Caribbean	Agricultural Crops	Y	X,M	Y	G	N	Y	NB	R

Case No.	Region	Sector	Questions							
			1	2	3	4	5	6	7	8
41.	Latin America	Business Services	N							
42.	Central America & Caribbean	Electrical Equipment	N							
43.	Asia	Misc. Manufactures	Y	X,M,B	?	G	Y	Y	NB	R
44.	Central America & Caribbean	Fish & Shellfish	Y	X,M	Y	G	Y	Y	NB	R
45.	Central America & Caribbean	Agricultural Crops	N							
46.	Asia	Chemicals	Y	X,M,B	Y	G	Y	N	BIND	NUSXD
47.	Asia	Business Services	N							
48.	Latin America	Paper Products	Y	X	NA	G	Y	Y	BIND	NUSXD
49.	Latin America	Finance & Insurance	N							
50.	Latin America	Petroleum Services	Y	M	Y	G	N	N	NB	R

Key:

Y	-	Yes
N	-	No
B	-	Balancing of exports and imports
X	-	Export Requirement
M	-	Restriction on Imports (inc. Local Content)
G	-	General TRIP Requirement
S	-	Specific to the Project
NB	-	Not Binding TRIP Requirement
BIND	-	Binding TRIP Requirement
ok	-	Approved by OPIC
R	-	Redundant
NXUS	-	No Significant Exports to U.S.
NUSXD	-	No Significant U.S. Exports Displaced
XUSDOUSM	-	Exports to U.S. Displace Other U.S. Imports
NA	-	Not Applicable
?	-	Unclear

Source: Overseas Private Investment Corporation

Table 9
OPIC SAMPLE
Summary

Percent Distribution of Projects:	
Central America & Caribbean	40%
Asia	24%
Africa	12%
Middle East	8%
Percent Projects Subject to TRIPS:	48%
Percent TRIP Projects Subject to:	
Local Content	21%
Export Minimum	29%
Both, or Balancing	50%
Percent TRIP Projects Subject to Numerical Requirements	29%
Percent TRIP Requirements Linked to Benefits:	63%
Percent TRIP Projects in which Requirements are Redundant	83%

Source: Overseas Private Investment Corporation

Assessment of the evidence about the characteristics and extent of TRIP requirements

(1) *Frequency.* The information on the frequency of TRIP requirements shows great variation. The most complete survey (1977 Commerce Benchmark) found only about 6 percent of U.S. overseas affiliates subject to TRIP requirements. The much narrower universe of all OPIC supported projects showed 40 percent subject to TRIP requirements, but TRIP and potential TRIP requirements were very broadly defined; the even more limited Guisinger survey found 51 percent subject to TRIP requirements.

(2) *Type of industry.* The incidence of TRIP requirements varies greatly by industry. The automotive sector is repeatedly found to be a principal target (27 percent of U.S. overseas affiliates surveyed in the Commerce Benchmark survey subject to some type of performance requirement, 75 percent of the Guisinger automotive sample, more than 80 percent of the ITC automotive sample). In the food processing industry, Guisinger's study found 48 percent subject to TRIP requirements. In chemicals and petrochemicals, Guisinger found a large number (unspecified) subject to TRIP requirements; the ITC study found 12 percent. In computers and office equipment, the ITC study found them to be infrequent and unimportant.

(3) *Type of Country.* Both developed countries and less developed countries use TRIP requirements. In terms of numbers of countries, LDC usage is more prevalent (48 percent of LDC's and 38 percent of the developed countries examined had TRIP requirements at least on the books in the USTR Computerized Inventory.) In terms of amount of investment in countries that use TRIP requirements, the developed countries, e.g. Canada, Australia, France, Spain, and Greece, had larger affiliate operations (72 percent of the total capital in a sample of 17 countries). The Guisinger study warns, moreover, that other developed countries use "implicit performance requirements" with the same objective as LDC TRIPs.

(4) *Type of TRIP Requirement.* In the USTR Computerized Inventory, it appears that local-content TRIP requirements are more frequent in LDCs than in developed countries. In automobiles and chemicals, local content requirements were generally more frequent than export minimums; in computers and office equipment, export minimums were more frequent (ITC study). Overall, in the USTR Computerized Inventory, it appears that about 40 percent of the

51

countries set numerical targets while 60 percent are negotiable or discretionary. Specific numerical targets are more often found in developing countries (50 percent), less in developed countries (18 percent). Forty-seven percent of the local-content type TRIP requirements appear to have specific numerical targets, 33 percent of the export type TRIP requirements are numerical. The sample of OPIC cases suggests that when TRIP requirements are used, combined export and import requirements and export and import balancing are frequent. Finally, the OPIC sample shows that when TRIP requirements are used, they are often linked to some form of favorable treatment (63 percent).

Impact of TRIP Requirements on Investment, Trade and U.S. Jobs

Only three of these studies attempted to measure the effects of TRIP requirements on investment behavior and trade patterns. These three are the ITC study, the study by Guisinger and associates, and the OPIC analysis.

The three studies employed the same methodology, but one of the studies (Guisinger and associates) points out a serious methodological weakness with this approach. The common methodology was to ask the investing firms how they would have altered their behavior (decision to invest, and subsequent pattern of imports and exports) if particular host countries had abandoned their particular performance requirements. Even if the answers could be taken to be exact, this compares the actual operations of firms with a hypothetical world in which the target countries have no performance requirements while all other countries are allowed to keep their locational policies for attracting investment intact. Since Guisinger and associates found intense competition for investment between countries, and substantial equivalency among policy tools, they labeled this methodological approach an "extreme" standard for judging the impact of any one performance requirement. The proper question to pose to the firms, they argued, was to ask how the firms would alter their behavior if a particular country relinquished its performance requirements and all other countries changed their locational inducements by an equivalent amount. When this question was asked, the answer varied considerably from how the firms replied to the "extreme" version. This same finding seemed to be present in the ITC study as well (see the response of the automotive industry).

A second methodological problem with these studies is that they asked hypothetical questions about which the investors may not have developed adequate cost information.

Study by the U.S. International Trade Commission on the Impact of Foreign Trade-Related Performance Requirements on U.S. Industry and Foreign Investment Abroad (1982)

The ITC study defined TRIP requirements as export minimums, import maximums, and local content rules. Respondents were asked to identify how many of their affiliates abroad were operating under TRIP requirements and which countries imposed the TRIP requirements. They were also asked whether the TRIP requirements played a large or a small role in the investment decision and whether they stimulated or hindered direct investment. The respondents were also asked to estimate the quantitative impact of TRIP requirements on their trade with their affiliates. The ITC investigators then used the Labor Department input-output model to translate the trade changes into changes in employment in the affected industries.

With regard to the impact of TRIP requirements:

(a) In the chemical industry, U.S. direct investment overseas was slightly retarded by the use of TRIP requirements and would have increased overall by $56.9 million in their absence. The existence of TRIP requirements was reportedly a relatively minor factor in the decision by one U.S. chemicals firm to invest in a foreign country. U.S. trade in 1981 was affected by performance requirements in that U.S. exports to affiliates of six respondents operating under TRIP requirements were lessened because of such requirements. Four of the respondents quantified this loss, reporting that in the absence of TRIP requirements in 1981, U.S. exports to eight countries (Brazil, Mexico, Spain, Republic of Korea, Peru, Indonesia, Columbia, and India) would have increased by $74.2 million (1.7 percent of respondents' total exports to their affiliates). The U.S. output loss translated into a total job loss of 605 positions in the chemical industry and in industries providing goods and services to the chemical sector.

(b) In the automotive sector, U.S. direct foreign investment was slightly enhanced by the use of TRIP requirements because investing firms were required to increase investment for host country production rather than import certain products. The existence of TRIP requirements appeared to most often be a minor factor in the decision by one U.S. motor-vehicle manufacturer to invest in a foreign country. Seven firms indicated that the absence of performance requirements in 1981 would have altered U.S. trade with their affiliates. However, only four firms indicated that U.S. exports would have increased to two other countries (Venezuela and Canada), for an overall increase of $48.7 million (0.9 percent of the automotive industry respondents' total export to their affiliates), while U.S. imports from two countries (Canada and Mexico) would have decreased by $59.6 million. Based on the estimated loss of U.S. exports and additional U.S. imports in 1981, U.S. production and employment in the motor vehicle and motor vehicle equipment industry was decreased by $144.3 million. This U.S. output loss translated into a total job loss of 2,008 positions in the motor vehicle and equipment industry and industries providing goods and services to that industry. However, three of the four U.S. motor vehicle manufacturers disputed the previous findings in general (with particular emphasis on Mexico). The three indicates that the absence of TRIP requirements would have resulted in lower U.S. exports because the use of TRIP requirements and accompanying investment incentives— particularly market protection—by a host country could allow U.S. firms a greater presence in that country than would an open market or alternate methods of encouraging domestic production, and therefore, in the absence of TRIP requirements, existing U.S. exports to these affiliates could be lost or reduced. They also argued that by encouraging the development of a domestic motor-vehicle industry through the use of TRIP requirements, a country created a market for U.S. exports of capital goods.

(c) In the office, computing, and accounting machine sector U.S. direct foreign investment in 1981 would have, in the absence of TRIP requirements, declined by $18.3 million in Mexico and $146,000 in Spain and increased by $1.2 million in Brazil, for an overall decrease of $17.2 million. In general, TRIP requirements were reported to have had only a minor effect on the decision to invest abroad. The reported effect of performance requirements on U.S. trade in 1981 was a small decrease in U.S. exports and a minuscule decrease in U.S. imports. Three firms surveyed indicated that the absence of TRIP requirements in 1981 would have altered U.S. trade with their affiliates. However, only two firms could quantify these changes, reporting that overall exports would have increased by \$13.6 million (0.5 percent of the sector respondents' total exports to their affiliates). Based on the estimated loss of both U.S. exports and U.S. imports in 1981, the U.S. output loss translated into a total job loss of 341 positions in this sector and in industries providing goods and services to this sector. It should be remembered that the ITC study apparently focused only on intra-firm trade effects.

The Study by Stephen Guisinger and Associates (1985)

Like the ITC study, the study by Stephen Guisinger and associates measured the "effectiveness" of performance requirements imposed on foreign investors by asking the latter to compare their behavior in a country under current incentive-and-disincentive policies with the hypothetical conditions that would prevail if that country removed its investment package and the investment packages of all other countries remained constant.

Labeling this an admittedly "extreme" methodology, the surveyors found:

(a) In two-thirds of the 74 cases surveyed, the choice of where to locate the investment was influenced by the incentive policies the host government did offer. Conversely, only one-third of the 74 projects passed the "extreme" test; that is, the investments would have been located in the same host country even if all incentives in that country had been removed beforehand while the investment attraction packages in other countries had remained intact. In this setting, the study discovered that host governments competed quite actively for potential foreign investors and could not reduce the appeal of their investment packages without losing substantial foreign investment. Interviews with government officials revealed considerable knowledge of investment packages offered elsewhere; moreover there appeared to be an appreciable follow-the-leader pattern in the effort to attract and shape the behavior of foreign firms.

(b) Direct subsidies to affect foreign investor location and operations were more prevalent in the developed countries, while trade protection to achieve the same ends was more frequent in the developing countries. From the firm's point of view, however, the authors calculated, there was a large measure of equivalency: a one-time tax-free cash grant of 50 percent of the value of an investment (Ireland, France), for example, is tantamount to a 30 percent annual effective rate of protection over the lifetime of an investment. For EC countries, there may be supplemental trade protection. Moreover, the data from Europe show an upward trend in the overall net cash equivalent of incentives to attract foreign corporate operations.

(c) While 38 of the 74 cases in the sample were subject to explicit TRIP requirements (and in some of the other cases the incentive packages were tied to trade performance), TRIP requirements were instrumental in altering the location in only four of 74 cases. "Altering" apparently meant the government required a different trade pattern for the firm if it wished to continue to produce or export to the country. No data are given on investments not made due to TRIP requirements.

(d) In the automobile sector, the TRIP requirements did increase exports and reduce imports of intermediate products. The authors hypothesize that mature technology makes the automobile industry somewhat "footloose". Domestic content is not an unattainable goal from either the host countries, or the foreign firms' point of view, even though it might affect the cost structure. In the computer industry, in contrast, TRIP requirements did not play an important role.

(e) In the food processing industry, where 12 out of 25 firms were subject to TRIP requirements, performance requirements (which include but are not limited to TRIP requirements) were seen to reduce total foreign investment.

(f) With regard to the petrochemical industry, the authors concluded that, because of the dominant importance of access to raw materials and to market demand in determining production location, the combined package of investment incentives and performance requirements did not have significant effect on the patterns of production and trade.

(g) In several of the 38 cases subject to TRIP requirements, corporate officials told the study team that their firms eventually would have achieved the specified levels of exports or domestic content on their own. The principal impact of the TRIPs was to "accelerate the firms' plans to develop local suppliers and enter export markets."

(h) There was a large degree of non-transparent and discretionary behavior on the part of countries that did not employ explicit TRIP requirements. The Industrial Development Authority in Ireland and the Economic Development Board in Singapore were cited as notable examples. In lieu of TRIPs, both agencies rewarded projects designed to meet trade performance objectives and withheld benefits from projects that did not. Instead of imposing domestic content and export-minimum requirements, both Ireland and Singapore exercised comparable leverage through discretionary incentive policies.

(i) Front-end cash grants, largely a feature of the European Economic Community, greatly facilitated investments by international companies "strapped" for funds. In one case, $500,000 of parent company new direct investment built and equipped a $50 million facility.

OPIC

The sample of OPIC projects suggest that in the great majority of cases the TRIP requirements were not binding (83 percent, Table 7), in the sense that the investor did not significantly alter his pattern of purchases or sales to meet the requirements. The typical responses for local content requirements were that it was either more economical to source domestically or that the sourcing requirement was negotiable, and that for export minimums it had been the investor's intention from the start to export part or all of his production. The redundancy of the TRIP requirements permitted OPIC to conclude that the TRIP requirements did not, per se, significantly affect the pattern of trade, and therefore did not reduce substantially the positive trade benefits the U.S. would gain from the investment.

In three of the four cases in which the TRIP requirements were considered binding (non-redundant), OPIC concluded that no significant amount of U.S. exports would be displaced. In the remaining case, the additional exports of the project to the U.S. would simply displace U.S. imports from other sources.

Thus no projects were rejected on TRIP requirement grounds.

U.S. and International Policy

The United States has a variety of instruments for dealing with foreign TRIP requirements should it be determined that they adversely affect U.S. trade or constitute significant obstacles to increased foreign direct investment.

Section 301 of the U.S. trade law, as amended in 1984, allows the President to challenge any foreign trade practice that he deems unfair, unjustifiable or discriminatory, and a burden to U.S. commerce. The 1984 amendment explicitly extends the scope of Section 301 to include TRIP requirements. If negotiations fail to eliminate the "offending" practice, the President is authorized to retaliate by withdrawing previous concessions or establishing new trade restrictions not limited to the sector or product at issue. A review of the 63 cases filed under Section 301 since 1975 indicates that none were directly concerned with TRIP requirements as we have defined them (i.e., specific to foreign-owned firms). Several, however, involved foreign government regulations that directed or encouraged all firms within their borders to purchase material or service inputs locally.

Section 307 of the Tariff and Trade Act of 1984 deals specifically with export requirements. If USTR finds that a foreign export requirement adversely affects U.S. economic interests, and if negotiations to remove the requirement fail, the President is authorized to undertake trade retaliation against that country. One case was brought against Taiwan, in the automotive sector, and a negotiated settlement was reached.

Also, as noted above, OPIC is required by law to decline insurance or finance for any project in which a TRIP requirement by the host country would "reduce substantially the positive trade benefits likely to accrue to the United States from the investment" (OPIC is also required to consider the U.S. employment effect and the environmental effects of all projects it contemplates supporting).

International Agreements and Treaties

TRIP requirements may be the subject of complaint under a number of GATT (General Agreement on Tariffs and Trade) provisions. The relevant provisions are those dealing with national treatment (Article III), elimination of quantitative restrictions (Article XI), subsidies (Article XVI and the Subsidies Code), and state trading enterprises (Article XVII).

Without attempting a legal analysis, it would appear that the national treatment article, which prohibits discrimination between imported and domestically produced goods, would prohibit special charges or taxes on foreign firms that fail to meet TRIP requirements (either minimum export or local content), and that the prohibition against quantitative mixing requirements would preclude local content requirements. A case could also be made that local content requirements, especially if stated in quantitative terms, are in effect a restraint on imported inputs other than tariffs. A further argument can be made that export requirements force the firm to subsidize exports from profits on domestic sales, thus amounting to a state-induced export subsidy (or state-induced dumping). If the export requirement is tied to investment incentives, the state indirectly provides the export subsidies. Export subsidies for primary products are not illegal if they do not result in more than an equitable share of world trade.

To summarize, it would appear that the United States has adequate authority under its own law and under GATT to challenge foreign TRIP requirements should it choose to do so. The United States is also responsible for placing TRIP requirements on the agenda for the Uruguay Round. In the Negotiating Group on Trade-Related Investment Measures subsequent to Punto del Este, the debate about the extent to which TRIPs affect trade patterns has continued at length, with the U.S. delegation espousing the argument that the effects are substantial, and others rebutting this contention. With regard to the negotiating proposals themselves, the United States, the EC, and Japan have limited themselves to the question of which GATT articles are appropriate to discipline which performance requirements, rather than the larger question of how to regulate investment incentive packages per se.

Conclusions

The empirical evidence suggests that TRIP requirements, while not attractive on economic efficiency grounds, are not a significant obstacle to increased foreign direct investment. The evidence on TRIP requirement frequency is not conclusive. The estimates of the extent to which TRIP requirements actually alter trade and investment patterns suggests that they have a small overall impact. In many cases TRIP requirements appear redundant. In those cases where they might be binding—i.e. raise costs and discourage investment—they are apt to be coupled with investment incentives, muting or canceling their investment discrimination effect. The U.S. government has tools to address the more egregious foreign TRIP requirements, should it choose to do so, but the urgency and importance of this task should not be exaggerated. The Uruguay Round may be a promising avenue for multinational control of TRIPs, especially if this approach ultimately leads to a broader effort to limit and regularize investment incentive packages in the North as well as in the South.[1]

---

[1]The pros and cons of different approaches to integrating TRIPs into the New GATT Round are spelled out in more detail in "Tread Carefully in the Field of TRIP Measures," *The World Economy*, Spring, 1988.

III. International Investment Policy: A View from the Private Sector

By Harvey E. Bale, Jr.

Introduction

American companies with global market interests, and, to a growing extent, their European and Japanese counterparts, increasingly believe that international investment issues have been undeservedly ignored and mired in political controversy for too long. A substantial proportion of international trade is carried out by "multinational" companies in the United States. This proportion is approximately 80 percent. And global resource allocation and financial conditions in many developing countries are increasingly dependent on the attraction of international direct investment flows. Correspondingly, international trade disputes will probably increasingly concern investment-related disputes in both goods and services activities.

Attempts at rule-making in the international investment field have been increasing, as bilateral and multilateral negotiating activity has accelerated in recent years. These efforts culminated in the GATT ministers decision to seek to reduce the distortions and barriers to expanding world trade and economic development through negotiations on trade-related investment measures.

Having spent a number of years working with the Office of the U.S. Trade Representative on a variety of investment-related initiatives and problems, it is a continuing strong interest of mine professionally to pay close attention to international investment issues. International trade and investment issues are of critical importance to the Hewlett-Packard Company, a major U.S. producer of computer equipment and systems, test and measurement equipment and medical instruments. While HP ranks in the top 50 largest U.S. corporations, it ranks seventh (1986) in its ratio of U.S. exports to worldwide sales at nearly 20 percent. HP also has a major investment commitment overseas, with a presence in more than 50 countries and manufacturing operations in more than 15 of them; and greater than 50 percent of HP's revenues are generated overseas. Thus, the global environment for trade in goods and services, investment and intellectual property is important to its performance.

The following discussion will, however, go beyond my own perspective of HP's interests to reflect what I personally believe are the more general concerns about international investment policy issues in that important segment of the U.S. business community having multinational interests.

Background

Business Attitudes Toward Performance Requirements

Government intervention in the cross-border flow of investment is commonly found both in many developed as well as less-developed countries. Indeed, some restrictions exist in all countries. Certain product sectors or activities may be off-limits (or restricted) to foreign investors, as is the case in the United States; on the other hand, all new investments or acquisitions may have to be "screened" for approval; foreigners may not enjoy some benefits, such as access to local government procurement, available to locally-owned firms; remittances of currency to the parent company may be severely restricted, even in countries that are experiencing serious balance of payments problems; also, foreign investors may be encouraged or forced to take on local partners who do not necessarily add value to the enterprise; or, they may be legally entitled to a majority equity position.

Finally, "performance requirements" frequently are applied to foreign investors that are often not applied to local investors. These take the form of local-content requirements; export requirements; trade-balancing requirements; technology transfer obligations; local licensing requirements on product distribution rights or patent royalties; manufacturing requirements; and global product-mandating requirements that require product development from the R&D stage through worldwide marketing.

I have often heard businessmen say that the non-performance requirement interventions by foreign governments mentioned above are far more significant barriers to foreign investment than are performance requirements. I tend to agree, at least as a short-term problem. Obstacles to the establishment of enterprises, remittance restrictions, and forced-minority equity positions are serious obstacles to the establishment of foreign investments.

Performance requirements, on the other hand, are usually subject to negotiation on an investment-project basis, with the understanding of both the investor and host-country government that if performance demands are too onerous, then any investment project will not go forward. Also, requirements of one type may sometimes be substituted for another during the negotiations between investor and local authorities, or during the actual implementation or operation of the new enterprise. Finally, local governments may "bribe" foreign investors to accept performance requirements, with financial incentive offerings. Thus, to a company contemplating the establishment of an enterprise in a foreign country, performance requirements may be just a "cost of doing business" compared to the other, more severe types of investment impediments. (Frequently, investors find that these costs are ratcheted up by the local government after the investment has been made; but this is only experienced once they are too deeply committed to readily pull back.)

Nevertheless, because regimes exacting performance requirements are not normally stable, and because they do impose additional costs and risks on investors, are usually discriminatorily applied, and are not transparent, foreign investors around the world tend to object to them in principle and consider them damaging to the global trading system. U.S. companies, in concert with organizations such as the Business Roundtable, the Emergency Committee for American Trade, and the U.S. Council for International Business, have taken the position that performance requirements constitute an important nontariff barrier and distortion to international trade and investment flows and should be negotiated away in GATT multilateral trade negotiations and in bilateral negotiations of trade and investment treaties. Most often cited problem countries that levy performance conditions as a requirement of foreign investment activity are the "newly-industrialized countries" of Asia and Latin America, and a few developed countries.

For an individual company, the tolerance of performance requirements can be quite high because of competitive pressures among firms for access to a host country market. Thus many companies will frequently negotiate the best possible terms, and then evaluate the feasibility of moving forward on an investment project. In such negotiations between investors and host-country governments, an advantage to the host in the ability to impose relatively more onerous requirements is held by countries with large internal markets, having the attractiveness of the local market and financial resources to offer in trade for local content and other obligations placed on investors.

The discrepancy between the philosophic and long-term economic reasons for multinational companies to be opposed to performance requirements on the one hand, and being forced to accommodate investment plans to current practices of many host developing countries on the other, creates an ambivalence on the part of U.S. executives toward performance requirements. The discrepancy cuts across sectoral lines, with automobile companies facing perhaps the greatest performance requirement challenges today and being most concerned about shifts in host country performance requirement policies—either to make them more onerous or to liberalize them (thereby possibly attracting new competitors previously dissuaded from entering the market by these requirements). Executives find that the continued viability of past investments are at stake in host countries, and therefore are sometimes reluctant to call for rapid reform or liberalization of onerous performance requirements. Thus, multinational companies are in a difficult position to take a strong leadership role in calling for liberalization of this type of trade distortion and investment barrier. Instead, they are reliant on the home-country government to take a strong leadership position on trade and investment liberalization. The main role of industry is then to provide information on problem areas including information on where rapid dismantling of these barriers and distortions might have harmful effects on companies and host countries.

U.S. Policy Precepts

Regardless of the dilemmas that American multinationals may face with respect to performance requirements, the federal government has its own reasons for addressing these types of foreign measures. The Office of the U.S. Trade Representative (USTR), the Commerce Department and other federal agencies concerned with trade and investment policies must represent the interests of the nation as a whole and those of various constituent groups. This means that the government must consider what effects performance requirements have on the development process in the LDCs that engage these measures and, at least as importantly, what effect these measures have on U.S.

employment and domestic production. Labor unions in this country have taken a strong position in opposition to foreign export and other performance requirements, arguing that they result in lost employment in the United States.

Foreign local content, technology transfer and export requirements certainly may substantially alter the direction of trade flows—indeed, that is often their purpose—and make overseas investment by U.S. companies increasingly controversial and subject to penalties in the future because of alleged net employment-outflow effects. The Reagan Administration position on performance requirements reflects the concerns that foreign performance requirements represent an obstacle to exports and can stimulate U.S. imports. In 1986, the Administration issued a policy statement reflecting this perspective by stating, in part:

> Local content requirements artificially displace imports, much as quotas do. Export requirements like export subsidies can artificially displace increase the supply of products in world markets, often at the expense of home country production and exports...
> [T]hese requirements distort trade and investment flows.

In 1986 the Administration initiated an "unfair trade" complaint against Taiwanese export performance requirement policies, using a recently-enacted (1984) law specifically passed by Congress to single out foreign export requirements for special attention and action by the USTR.

Finally, the Administration has made "trade-related investment measures" a topic for discussion and negotiation in the Uruguay Round of multilateral trade negotiations (MTN). The issue is on the agenda despite the general opposition to its consideration by most LDCs, especially the NICs.

The discussion toward the end of this paper will return to consider the question of appropriate U.S. policies toward these performance requirements measures.

Why Performance Requirements?

If initiatives to address performance requirements are to be seriously pursued, an understanding of the rationale for them is important. The discussion here attempts to explain their occurrence by

65

describing the conditions that appear to me to have contributed most to their frequency. Most of the explanations that I have seen appear to have been directed toward providing theoretical defenses, and do not sufficiently reflect the protectionist forces behind them. I think that the major factors underlying the presence of performance requirements are: (1) allegedly distorted MNC trading patterns; (2) local-industry protection; (3) MNC-host government collusion; (4) balance of payments problems; and (5) industrial development objectives. Time and space allow only a brief explanation of each of these categories, and I should add that these factors do not appear often individually or to the exclusion of each other.

MNC Trade Patterns

One of the assertions that host-government officials sometime make for commonly-found local content and export requirements is that multinational companies export less and import more than do locally-owned companies. In one East-Asian advanced developing country, until recently, U.S. companies were required to export 50 percent of their output, with the justification that this represented the national ratio of industrial exports to sales! Also, the government of one major developed country claimed that foreign-owned companies typically import proportionately more than do local firms. A question not addressed was whether those foreign companies (mostly American-based) also export more; instead, the government's investment screening agency and its apologists simply asserted that they do not.

The underlying argument for these perceptions of multinational company trade behavior is that the key strategic decisions on production and trade are made outside of the host country's borders and these decisions reflect factors such as global marketing objectives assigned to various divisions in the MNC as well as international tax and other regulatory policies. Thus, MNCs will "under-export" because it does not want competition with itself; meanwhile, it will tend, so the argument goes, to import "excessively" from overseas affiliates. Local-content and export requirements are seen, therefore, as corrective policies.

Because multinational companies operate in many countries, they do tend to develop worldwide sources for products to market and as inputs. The problems of price and quality tend to dictate limited global sourcing options in the short run. But, the same global sourcing attributes that may tend to result in large imports also offers global marketing channels for products made in host country markets. In fact, the bringing of international trade experience to a host country is one of the principal advantages of MNCs to developing countries seeking to develop overseas markets for local products. Therefore, MNCs can be important vehicles of export-led growth for LDCs.

Further, foreign-owned companies are sensitive to the role they play in the host country, particularly in LDCs. The general view of MNCs as rapacious invaders is certainly no longer true, if it ever was generally valid. The MNCs in manufacturing that this author is familiar with seek to contribute local production, technology, quality development, employment and training opportunities that are typically more beneficial and durable than the effects of the forced local-sourcing that is too often prevalent in many countries. In fact, MNCs have reason to be much more sensitive to local economic goals, as "guests," than do local investors. In a number of the foreign investment approval processes that this writer has been aware of in detail as a U.S. trade policy official, foreign investment approval agencies have been under pressure to reject or heavily regulate (with performance requirements) the U.S. investor in favor of a local investor who planned to do little in the way of adding real value to the development of the local economy. Headquarters and local managers of MNCs know that unless their company is seen as a "good citizen" by the local government and population, it is at risk and, further, will find its success limited by its inaction on local national goals. On the other hand, the fact is that local investors often are not as inclined, frankly, to be as sensitive to these matters.

In sum, there appears to be no evidence that this explanation or rationalization for performance requirements is very convincing even though it is frequently encountered. It should be added, however, that there might be a difference between the behavior of U.S.-based and Japan-based multinationals, in which the latter appear to tie their overseas patterns of trade more closely for a longer period of time to business partners in Japan. This seems to be an extension of the "longstanding-relationship" principle that binds Japanese firms together.

Protection of Local Industry

This writer believes that at the core of the occurrence of restrictive investment policies and performance requirements measures is the simple protectionist impulse in favor of local industry. Export performance requirements, while justified on the grounds discussed above or for balance of payments reasons (discussed below), conveniently restrict the supply of the output of MNCs to the local market, and lessen the competition to locally-owned firms. The example mentioned above of the 50 percent export requirements in a certain Asian country was a case of this kind, i.e., local producers did not want competition from MNCs and lobbied to have at least half of MNCs' output exported. Local content requirements are also a means for local governments to appease and ingratiate themselves to powerful local business groups. Such requirements act as quotas against imports. Regardless of the quality of local production, which will be discouraged from improving by the protectionism of these quota-like provisions, MNCs must find—and source from—local vendors.

In this light, LDCs making heavy use of performance requirements place a drag on their economy. And when performance requirements are tied to financial incentives, the policy becomes even more burdensome on the rest of the economy, since it is subsidizing inefficiency indirectly via offsetting the costs of it to MNCs.

Host Government/MNC Collusion

A variation of the inefficiency created by local content and export requirements is the possible cooperation between host governments and MNCs, by which the firm itself may offer to accept various types of performance requirements in return for a monopoly position (or incentives) in the local market, *including protection against imports,* for a lengthy time period.

The deal involves the host country achieving its objective of attracting the foreign investor coupled with apparent "benefits" involving the requirements, while the firm gets monopoly rents in excess of the amount necessary to pay the costs of the requirements. Left out of the market, of course, are other competitors—American, Japanese and European. Of course, once the investment is made, the host government may change the terms of the agreement it made with the "monopoly" foreign investor. This has happened often when the host government believes that the deal was imbalanced, the government changes, or global or local market conditions change.

A host government/MNC deal of this kind creates an unfortunate force for prolonged protection in the host country, where the firm is enjoying a benefit; this can be costly to the host country and put in conflict with the home country of the MNC which might be interested in seeking liberalization of trade barriers for its home-country products. It does not appear that many investors in many industries become engaged in these types of protectionist deals, though if initial capital costs are very large relative to the market, and economies of scale are substantial, then the likelihood may arise for the negotiation of monopoly or near-monopoly arrangements. Host-countries should avoid these deals, and MNCs stand to lose their favored status in the long run anyway.

Industrial Development and Balance of Payments

Two of the most frequent reasons presented for performance requirements are that they constitute part of a host country's industrial policy and a program to avoid a deterioration in the host country's balance of payments. These are very large and complex topics by themselves, and this section treats only briefly a few problems with these rationales for performance requirements.

Concerning the argued contribution of performance (particularly local content) requirements to industrial development, the argument usually briefly runs as follows: while it may be accepted (though by no means fully or universally by LDC techno- and bureaucrats) that foreign direct investment brings capital, technology and skill training in activities with global market application, the contributions of this investment to host-country development can be further skewed or augmented by requiring foreign companies to encourage the expansion of industrial activity by forcing linkages via required purchases from local suppliers. After all, local content requirements are akin to the import restrictions permitted by GATT Article XVIII concerning infant industry protection.

A problem with this argument is that local production is being fostered by policies that are also like the general and costly import-substitution policies of the 1960s and 1970s now discouraged in favor of export-oriented policies. Furthermore, the restrictions are quantitative barriers to imports, and are more costly than tariffs for the host country. Also, it is frequently the case that local entrepreneurs in competition with the MNCs in a host country are far less burdened with performance requirements. Thus, foreign companies often face local competition that is not constrained to use domestic sources for inputs. (Indeed, the local competition may also be the only source for the foreign investor's inputs!) This writer's view is, briefly, that local content requirements are less a tool for industrialization than a vehicle to reward domestic constituents of local officials.

A recent IMF staff research paper argued similarly that export and local content requirements "are similar to trade restrictions, in that they create an implicit subsidy to exports and import substitution, and have similar disadvantages, in that they distort resource allocation, can lead to the development of an inefficient industrial base that is unable to compete without such protection, and can invite trade retaliation."

Local content, export and trade or foreign exchange balancing requirements often have a balance of payments justification. MNCs, it is argued, should not be allowed to use scarce foreign exchange or to drive the exchange rate down by actions involving importation or earnings remittances. Often, exports must be *at least* 100 percent of the value of imports or foreign exchange use of the foreign investor. It is also frequently true that the exports of the foreign investor must be a product of the firm's operation, rather than a product that is unrelated to the firm's activity—even though there may be no comparative advantage in exporting the firm's products. The firm's local sales (again, not infrequently protected) tend to subsidize losses on foreign sales in such circumstances.

That host countries should consider balance of payments in applying performance requirements is a phenomenon that does almost nothing positive to overcome the other negative elements driving a balance of payments problem. On the contrary, it is something that surely is negative for attracting and expanding foreign activity. Such activity could ultimately contribute positively to restoring healthy external payments conditions and economic growth.

The Problems of Attitude and Anti-Democratic Politics

Performance requirements and other forms of direct investment restrictions reflect two basic problems in the attitudes and politics relating to foreign investment in those countries imposing such restraints. One is the failure to appreciate the non-zero gains or "win-win" result of foreign direct investment for both home and host countries, particularly for debt-ridden LDCs. On this subject I quote the observations of the Brazilian businessman and politician Roberto Campos of just a couple of years ago on prevailing domestic political attitudes towards foreign investment in Brazil:

> The fashionable demons today are the multinational enterprises. Little does it matter that the state (Sao Paolo) most "spoiled" by the multinationals is also the richest...and that Piaui, untouched by them, is poor and dependent. The contrast between these two states reminds me of what Professor Joan Robinson of Cambridge said, with the notorious frankness of the Marxists "there is only one thing worse than being exploited, and that is not being exploited."
>
> ...
>
> Curiously, the American unions perceive the situation otherwise: they accuse the multinationals of benefiting other countries by exporting jobs! If the multinationals deserted us—which is not an impossibility if inflation, the exchange crisis, and the constant changing of the rules of the game become our style of life—we would not cure old sadnesses but would instead create new ills. Only our ideologues would possess the imagination to create new scapegoats in such a case.
>
> ...
>
> Developing countries are no longer—if they ever were—the paradise of the multinationals. The United States has become the magnet for European and Japanese investors precisely because they have two things we lack—a strong currency and stable rules of the game. As mentor of a good number of the technocrats, I would even give these ideologues technical assistance in this operation of "multicide"— the genocide of the multinationals—if they convinced me that this would enrich the country, bring social justice, produce more jobs and solve our foreign exchange crisis.

The two accompanying tables demonstrate Campos' point that developed country investors are not queuing at the door of LDCs to get in to make investments. Table 1 shows that OECD countries' direct investment flows to developing countries essentially leveled off in nominal terms after 1975, with the proportion of private direct capital constituting a significantly declining percentage of total private capital flows after 1970. The revival of this percentage after 1984 reflects the scarcity of private bank lending. More importantly, the regional destination for those direct investment flows appears to be increasingly concentrated in the Asian NICs, as indicated by the distribution of the stock of U.S. direct investment shown in Table 2.

The foreign investment policies of many developing countries (and some developed ones too) reflect more than just the victory of ideology over rationalism. They also represent the conquest of special interest groups (local businessmen who want protection from MNC competition or special benefits from their presence) over democratic economic interests. State intervention in the area of investment activities is a vehicle to block or manipulate foreign investment flows to favor narrow local interests able to use government regulation to foster their own enhancement. It is an anti-democratic process.

Table I

Private Capital Flows to Developing Countries from OECD Countries,1965-1986
($ billion)

Year	Total Private	Direct Investment	Direct as Pct. of Total
1965	$4.l	$2.5	61%
1966	4.0	2.2	55%
1967	4.4	2.1	48%
1968	6.4	3.0	47%
1969	6.6	2.9	44%
1970	9.8	3.7	38%
1971	10.3	3.3	32%
1972	10.7	4.2	39%
1973	17.3	4.7	27%
1974	15.4	1.9	12%
1975	29.1	11.4	39%
1976	30.4	8.3	27%
1977	39.1	9.8	25%
1978	50.6	11.6	23%
1979	49.6	13.4	27%
1980	40.4	9.8	24%
1981	55.5	15.8	28%
1982	46.4	10.3	22%
1983	35.0	7.8	22%
1984	42.5	11.1	26%
1985	10.2	6.7	66%
1986	23.0	11.8	51%

Source: OECD. Development Assistance Committee, *Development Cooperation: 1987 Report* (Paris, 1988)

Table 2
Regional Distribution of U.S. Foreign Direct Investment
($ billion or percent)

	1950	1966	1977	1980	1986
World	$11.8	$51.8	$146.0	$215.4	$260.0
	(100%)	(100%)	(100%)	(100%)	(100%)
Dev. Countries:	48.3%	68.1%	75.4%	73.5%	74.9%
Canada	30.4	30.3	24.0	20.9	19.3
Europe	14.7	31.6	42.8	44.7	47.4
Japan	0.2	1.4	3.1	2.9	4.4
LDC's:	48.7%	26.8%	21.8%	24.7%	23.3%
South/Central America	37.7	16.6	12.0	12.3	10.8
Mexico	3.5	2.6	2.2	2.8	1.9
Brazil	5.5	1.7	4.0	3.6	3.5
Argentina	3.0	1.5	0.9	1.2	1.1
Venezuela	8.4	4.1	1.0	0.9	0.7
Africa	1.2	2.6	1.4	1.8	1.6
Middle East	5.9	2.8	-2.2	1.0	2.1
Asia/Pacific	2.7	2.5	3.8	3.9	6.2

Source: Office of Trade and Investment Analysis, International Trade Administration, U.S. Department of Commerce, *International Direct Investment: Global Trends and the U.S. Role,* Vol. II, forthcoming.

Controlled Versus Open Economies

The discussion above of political attitudes toward foreign investment attracts me to raise for brief discussion two skeletal models of foreign business environments in which foreign investment policies fit in consistently with trade, exchange-rate and tax policies. Restrictive investment policies frequently correspond to restrictive trade and burdensome tax policies in "controlled market" economies, whereas in "open market" countries, the opposing set of policies tend to be found. That is, there tend to be few investment restrictions, low trade barriers, lower taxes and more competitive exchange rates. The two models are juxtaposed in the following chart.

U.S. companies can be found operating in both types of environments; however, the corresponding business strategies and degrees of company resource commitment tend to differ substantially. Multinational companies tend to view open market economies, such as Singapore, as areas in which commitments tend to be made that will integrate operations in them into parts of the companies' *global* strategies of production, R&D and marketing. In short, companies tend to search for ways to grow in such environments, with resulting benefits to the local economy of inflows of capital, training and technology. In contrast, many companies will tend to do what is only required to meet the onerous regulations in controlled economies, hoping that the environment will improve later. Thus, a "presence" is often established in controlled economies, but a "commitment" to such a market will tend to be given a lower priority; this is extremely unfortunate for many countries, but companies are really faced with no other option if they are to remain competitive globally.

Table 3
Two Models of Foreign Business Environments

GOVERNMENT POLICY:

		I. Controlled	II. Open
A.	Fundamental Attitude Toward Domestic Market	•Control Access •Tolerate Foreign Firms Grudgingly	•Induce Market Participation by Competitive Firms
B.	General Policy Framework	•Protectionism •Foreign Investor Discrimination	•Open Access to Domestic Market •General Lack of Foreign Investor Discrimination
C.	Measures	•High Tariffs, Import Licensing, Quotas •Hidden Trade Barriers (e.g., Technical Standards •Investment Screening & Performance Requirements •Strict Buy-National Policies •Overvalued Exchange Rate •Burdensome Business Income Taxes	•Low Tariffs Aimed at Revenues •Few Quantitative Import Controls •Only Sectoral Foreign Investment Barriers •Tax Incentives for R&D and Manufacturing •Competitive Exchange Rate
D.	Policy Success Requirements	•Attraction of Large Local Market	•Development of Internationally Competitive Local Industry

Table 3 (continued)

BUSINESS RESPONSE:

A.	Basic Strategy	•Aimed to Achieve Regulations •Minimalist Approach to Domestic R&D and Manufacturing	•Maximize Presence to Reap Local Advantages •Include Local Manufacturing in Global Firm Plan
B.	Business Plan Objectives and Criteria for Success	•Maximize Local Market Share to Achieve ROI •Minimize New Capital to Minimize Political Risks	•Push for Efficient Operations •Aim at Global and Local Markets •Do Research and Development of Producs Locally

Where Should We Go From Here?

Given the simultaneous existence of investment, trade and other obstacles to the industrial growth in many countries, dealing in isolation with investment barriers would resolve neither companies' nor governments' concerns with such obstacles. However, addressing investment issues, such as has occurred over the last several years, brings to the fore matters that are important to the health of the global economy.

Policy initiatives in the area of foreign investment issues have not been lacking in the last few years. In the opinion of this author, these initiatives, referred to in more detail below, have been a major positive force for improving the operation of the international trading system. With the surge of debt and protectionist problems in the 1980s, the focus on the creation of new wealth via international investment and related technology flows promises to lay a better foundation for international trade and growth in the next decade. However, the requirements to address effectively the barriers to increased international investment flows include continued strong resolve against reactionary attitudes of autarky and market control by governments— attitudes that still prevail in many countries today. Also required is a continued growth of understanding of the role of international investment even by developed, capital-exporting-country negotiators.

What is clear is that government officials show continued lack of appreciation for the simultaneous export-creating and import-substituting effects that arise out of the wealth-creating effects of direct investment flows.

The Reagan Administration, with strong support by the Congress, has launched several efforts to liberalize foreign investment policies abroad while seeking to reduce the burdens of U.S. laws on foreign investors in the United States, such as state unitary tax rules. These include GATT action to negotiate on "trade-related investment measures," to find illegal the use of local content requirements in Canada, the negotiation of bilateral investment treaties with some developing countries, and the use of unfair trade statutes (e.g., Sections 301 and 307) in the cases of Brazilian and Taiwanese investment practices. Congress in the Trade Act of 1984 defined foreign investment barriers both as a category of unfair trade restrictions and as an important international trade negotiating objective of the United States.

\Progress has been made in recent years in achieving the liberalization of investment policies in Japan, Korea, China and Taiwan and in Canada (well before the conclusion of the recently-signed "free trade agreement"). The Administration's bilateral investment treaty program has recently received a boost by the congressional ratification of eight treaties. However, looking ahead, the United States government faces serious challenges to achieving further results from its initiatives in GATT and bilaterally that were undertaken in recent years. The U.S. government still lacks a clear vision of a strategy for accomplishing its objectives (or even what exactly the latter are) in the GATT and other negotiations on investment policies.

The increasing flow of foreign investment into the United States has put the Administration on the defensive in its maintenance of a policy favoring no investment restrictions. In addition, the investment portion of the Canadian "free trade agreement" may undercut current policy to liberalize investment practices abroad and to maintain an open foreign investment policy at home. (This is because the FTA, in a break with previous U.S. policy and distinct from U.S. demands of less-developed countries, permits Canada an unprecedented right to continue to screen significant acquisitions by foreign investors; to employ such performance requirements (e.g., technology transfers) that the United States is asking its GATT partners to give up; and to expropriate investments in the "cultural sector" without "public purpose," again in contradiction to the long-standing U.S. position on expropriations).

GATT Negotiations on Trade-Related Investment Measures

The United States has laid out an ambitious agenda for the Uruguay Round of Multilateral Trade Negotiations (MTNs) under GATT auspices. The list of targeted trade-distorting investment practices includes performance requirements, screening measures and investment incentives (a form of production subsidy that affects the pattern of trade by directly influencing the location of production).

The United States, and developing countries (notwithstanding their current practices) could achieve much progress in liberalization of a range of trade and trade-related measures this Round. However, the United States faces strong opposition from the major LDCs (e.g., Brazil, India) and has little support from the other OECD countries, except for Japan (today's leading capital exporter). The United States only succeeded in getting investment on the GATT negotiating agenda by Ambassador Clayton Yeutter's personal doggedness in the late hours of the last day of the Punte del Este ministerial conference that set the Uruguay Round agenda in 1986.

A major problem is that it is not only the LDCs that are "sinners" in the area of all three categories of trade-distorting investment measures noted above; but so are many of the OECD countries, including the United States insofar as incentives are concerned. In Canada, Europe, Japan and Australia there are significant screening measures and local content and technology transfer policies, especially tied to investment incentives or access to certain local markets (e.g., government procurement). It is questionable whether, in the way the negotiations are broken down into specific negotiating groups (investment, services, procurement, etc.)—that real progress can be made. The United States has not yet considered the trade-offs that would be necessary to make significant gains in this area, and whether it would be willing itself to make them. There is little leverage that it has within the investment area itself, and, furthermore, is threatening to reverse its own position in favor of liberal investment policies (see further below for more discussion on this).

"What if" (a popular question within Hewlett-Packard) the United States were able to make significant progress in the Uruguay

Round? What might be sought within the realm of the possible and desirable?

First, there should be an agreement among OECD countries that all trade-distorting performance requirements are to be prohibited. Not only should requirements to source locally, etc., be covered, but the mandatory requirements to invest abroad in order to sell into the government procurement market should also be covered. This does not mean that preferential discrimination on a price basis in favor of local producers (whatever their nationality of ownership) be given, absent a government procurement understanding. But companies should not have to locate production and research facilities in a developed-country market in order to merely *qualify* to sell to national and local governments. This is a large and growing investment and trade problem that also limits access to developed country government procurement markets for LDCs as well. It might be worthwhile, indeed, to consider merging the government procurement and investment negotiations, since the problems are related. That is, on the one hand, in the investment negotiations the problems of trade-distorting investment policies are being addressed; while in the government procurement negotiations, the problems of the distorting effects of discretionary government purchases on moving plants across borders is being tackled.

With respect to developing country practices, there should be a phase-out of performance requirements to allow LDCs to develop alternative (and better) policies to replace them; or, at least, there should be an agreement that Article XVIII's "infant industry" procedures should be rigorously followed. Thus, when the GATT's Contracting Parties do not find that the performance requirements in place or proposed by individual LDCs meet the objectives of GATT and objective economic development tests, then they should be eliminated as quickly as possible.

Bilateral Initiatives

The United States should continue to explore the opportunities to negotiate bilateral investment treaties with interested LDCs, since the model text provides much of what would be beneficial to such countries' ability to attract needed foreign investment. Concluded treaties with Egypt, Turkey and eight or so other countries are good models for the principles that American, European and Japanese foreign investors factor in, in evaluating LDC investment climates. Since the model was developed some seven years ago, consideration should now be given to reviewing its provisions and the degree of negotiating flexibility to be attached.

There seems little radical that needs to be performed on the text, but the performance requirement coverage might be broadened to be consistent with the U.S. GATT positions; at the same time, some additional flexibility, e.g., on dispute settlement, might be considered with some countries, like China, that have little or no experience, or cannot accept the U.S. approach at all. Some compromise on the scope of some provisions might be warranted, without giving up key points.

It will be interesting to see the fallout of the U.S.-Canada "free trade agreement" provisions on investment. In that agreement there are no investor-based dispute settlement rules, screening is sanctioned, many performance requirements are permitted (indirectly including export requirements, which are supposed to be banned by the agreement), and expropriation is now sanctioned for private-benefit purposes (contrary to U.S. policy and international law).

In future bilateral trade agreements, investment provisions should be included, as in the Canada and Israel treaties. Singapore and other ASEAN countries would be good potential candidates for concluding sound investment agreements as part of broader free trade deals.

Unilateral U.S. Policy Action on Investment Issues

Negotiations under the GATT, or bilaterally, are not the only possible means that the Administration has considered for addressing foreign investment practices.

Since 1985, the Administration has responded to the urgings of the Congress and major elements of the U.S. business community to take a more "aggressive" unilateral position toward "unfair trade practices"—i.e., those that, according to Section 301 of U.S. trade law, burden U.S. commerce and are unjustifiable, unreasonable and discriminatory. (Only tariffs fall generally outside this category fairly consistently.) The Administration has initiated Section 301 cases against foreign investment restrictions abroad, including export requirement measures in Taiwan and insurance industry restrictions in Korea. Pressures to unilaterally employ Section 301 and other possible unfair trade practice provisions (e.g., Section 307) of U.S. laws are likely to continue, if not grow.

81

There is a risk, however, that the United States will turn away from pursuing more liberal investment policies abroad because of the domestic negative reaction of some politicians, media writers and businessmen to the substantial growth of foreign investment in the United States. Such a turn would be for the worse for the long-term economic interests of both this country and developing countries that would regard the U.S. reaction as justification for their own restrictions on inward investment. The only significant reason for U.S. restrictions against foreign investors (besides an occasional national security concern) is a "reciprocity" action to prevent hostile takeovers by foreign firms whose home governments do not permit U.S. companies to counterattack by bidding to acquire the predator. A number of developed countries allow their multinational firms to make acquisitions from behind protective barriers against their own potential acquisition. This kind of market interference could, unless gradually phased out in OECD countries, help undermine a currently "open" U.S. investment policy.

Otherwise, the United States needs to continue to set a strong example for developing countries (as well as fundamentally not weaken its own economy) that open and expanding investment opportunities are advantageous for both capital exporting and importing countries.

References

Bale, H. E., "The U.S. Federal Government's Policy Towards Foreign Direct Investment," in Fry, E.H. and Radebaugh, L.H., eds., *Regulation of Foreign Direct Investment in Canada and the United States* (Provo: Brigham Young University Press, 1983).

Bale, H. E., "Trade Policy Aspects of International Direct Investment Policies," in Baldwin, R., ed., *Recent Issues and Initiatives in U.S. Trade Policy* (Cambridge: National Bureau of Economic Research, 1984).

Bale, H. E., "Foreign Investment Policy." Paper for the NOMOS Project Seminar II, Center for International Affairs, Harvard University, May 24, 1984. (Mimeo)

Bale, H. E., "The United States Policy Toward Inward Foreign Direct Investment," 18 *Vanderbilt Journal of Transnational Law* (Spring 1985).

Bale, H. E. and Walters, D. A., "Investment Policy Aspects of U.S. and Global Trade Interests," *Looking Ahead*, National Planning Association, January 1986.

Business Roundtable, *International Investment: A Plan for Action*, New York, April 1983.

Campos, R., Speech reprinted in *O Estado de Sao Paulo*, Sao Paulo, Brazil, June 9, 1983.

International Monetary Fund, Research Department, *Foreign Private Investment in Developing Countries*, Occasional Paper No. 33 (January 1985).

Moran, T. H. and Pearson, C., "Trade Related Investment Performance Requirements," A Study Prepared for the Overseas Private Investment Corporation, Washington, March 1987.

Office of the U.S. Trade Representative, *Model Treaty Concerning the Reciprocal Encouragement and Protection of Investment*, Revised, February 24, 1984.

Office of the U.S. Trade Representative, "Barriers to Investment," October 25, 1985. (Mimeo)

Organization for Economic Cooperation and Development, *Controls and Impediments Affecting Inward Direct Investment in OECD Countries*, Paris, 1987.

Organization for Economic Cooperation and Development, Development Assistance Committee, *Development Cooperation Review 1987*, Paris, 1987.

U.S. Department of Commerce, International Trade Administration, *International Direct Investment: Global Trends and the U.S. Role*, August 1984.

IV. FOREIGN DIRECT INVESTMENT IN HEAVILY INDEBTED DEVELOPING COUNTRIES: A VIEW FROM THE FINANCIAL COMMUNITY

*By Rimmer de Vries**

Introduction

Foreign direct investment has an important role to play in the financial rehabilitation and economic development of the middle-income, debt-burdened LDCs. This role is to become a catalyst for the reallocation of their abundant natural and human resources—away from inefficient uses that are a drain on domestic savings and foreign-exchange earnings, and toward industries that will absorb surplus labor, transfer technology and management skills, and open up new export markets.

This role is one that foreign investment has not often been called to play in recent decades. Multinational corporations were attracted to the larger debtor countries (Argentina, Brazil, Mexico, the Philippines, and Venezuela) in the 1960s and 1970s, mostly by the prospect of setting up industries geared to expanding domestic markets that were sheltered from foreign competition. To the smaller countries of Central and South America, foreign companies frequently came with the hope of serving growing regional markets such as the Central American Common Market and the Andean Pact that were likewise sheltered.

These investments were welcomed at first because they supported a process of rapid industrialization meant to be spearheaded by large privately owned companies and state-run corporations. In retrospect, the strategy was flawed because industry, pampered as it was with

* The author acknowledges the valuable assistance, in preparing this article, of members of his staff, particularly: Norman R. Klath, V.P., James M. Nash, V.P., Arturo C. Porzecanski, V.P., and Romualdo A. Roldan, V.P.

endless protectionism and burdened with extensive government regulation, did not develop the cost discipline, productivity, quality control, or scale economies necessary to outgrow the local market and compete in the world. Only recently, and in the wake of steep currency devaluations and austerity plans that cut consumer demand and labor costs, has there been a significant increase in the export orientation of multinational and local industries in the debtor LDCs.

The challenge ahead for all of the heavily-indebted LDCs is to build upon this relatively brief experience with export orientation, consolidating it in preparation for the eventual recuperation in domestic demand. This entails nothing less than the implementation of a new development strategy of outward-looking—rather than inward-looking—industrialization, the main elements of which are reforms of the public sector, the trade regime, and the financial system.

Public-sector reform is necessary for two reasons: first, to deregulate markets, so that prices may signal true scarcities rather than the preferences of politicians and government bureaucrats; and, second, to force state-owned companies to become competitive, in order to improve the savings performance of the government and the productivity of public-sector investments.

In all of the debtor countries with the notable exception of Chile, government intervention in labor, capital, and foreign exchange markets is pervasive and there is an abundance of state-owned companies with little chance of becoming and then remaining profitable. The private sector is subject to price controls, licensing requirements, and other forms of government intervention—always for the sake of worthwhile social goals, but at a high cost in terms of the performance of established concerns and the climate for new business ventures. State-owned companies, meanwhile, face untenable cost structures which cannot be altered because of political meddling in pricing, hiring, compensation, and other management prerogatives. These companies constitute a heavy drain on tax and credit resources and need to be closed down or broken up and privatized. Mexico and Argentina are now taking the first steps of such a rationalization process, but key countries such as Brazil and Venezuela have yet to begin.

Foreign trade regimes in all but two of the major debtors (Chile and Mexico) are badly in need of liberalization. Without it, industries will remain hampered by lack of access to raw materials, capital goods, and component parts at the lowest world prices, quickly losing competitiveness once the current degree of currency depreciation and domestic demand compression is lessened. Quantitative restrictions need to be abolished and tariffs lowered and made more uniform.

The domestic financial systems of the debtor LDCs, with the sole exception of Chile, are not functioning in a manner that can underwrite the expansion of productive investment. Capital markets are undeveloped, distorted, or segmented because of overregulation, especially of interest rates, and because of severe crowding out due to heavy public-sector borrowing requirements. As a result, financial savings in virtually all the debtor LDCs are unduly low, and credit to the private sector is costly and inefficiently allocated. The relationship between risks and rewards often favors capital flight— and seldom the repatriation of savings held abroad. Financial system reform is imperative to enable industries with a future to have access to funding at the lowest possible cost.

It is in a context of structural adjustment and sounder demand management policies that foreign direct investment can be expected to make a significant contribution to meeting the debtor countries' growth and foreign exchange needs. Multinational corporations can be encouraged to help buy into companies being privatized, set up export-oriented plants, and modernize financial institutions—and can be expected to respond even better than they already are doing in a small and distant country like Chile. The involvement of new investors can hasten the transition from a development strategy that is no longer adequate for the heavily indebted countries, to another which is.

The Imperative for Self Help

In the six years since the outbreak of the debt crisis, most of the afflicted countries have yet to achieve and sustain a combination of satisfactory economic growth, low inflation, and a strong balance of payments. Lack of external financing forced countries to undertake crash austerity policies and currency devaluations which have cut import dependence and improved current account performance. It has proven hard, nevertheless, to sustain demand management policies and start structural reforms, largely because of internal political constraints. External indebtedness is now higher relative to export proceeds than at the onset of the debt crisis because exports have not grown (see Table 1). Ratios of interest payments to exports, meanwhile,

Table 1
Ratio of external debt to exports
(goods, services and private transfers)

	1982	1985	1986	1987	% change in exports 1982 to 1987
Argentina	421	483	579	637	-14
Brazill	339	351	426	403	23
Chile	333	440	395	326	26
Colombia	184	257	191	217	38
Mexico	299	323	413	343	8
Nigeria	99	165	335	332	-41
Philippines	331	375	343	316	15
Venezuela	176	207	299	273	-36
Total	290	319	393	372	-14.8

Table 2
Ratio of interest payments to exports
(goods, services and private transfers)

	1982	1985	1986	1987
Argentina	50	50	49	49
Brazil	53	38	40	32
Chile	44	41	36	25
Colombia	22	25	18	19
Mcxico	44	34	35	27
Nigeria	8	10	17	22
Philippines	24	27	23	23
Venezuela	18	23	27	21
Total	35	32	33	28

have dropped but only because of a factor beyond the control of the debtor countries, namely, lower Eurocurrency interest rates (see Table 2).

Disappointing economic performance in the debtor countries has confirmed to commercial banks in the industrial countries the worst of their fears that first arose in 1982 and led to the abrupt slowdown in lending. In recent years, the banks have taken precautionary measures such as boosting their capital base and loan-loss reserves. U.S. money center banks, for example, increased their capital and reserves by 70 percent in the five years since the end of 1982. While new loans have been granted to countries needing financing in the context of IMF-supervised adjustment programs, banks have attempted to contain the growth of their overall exposure to the debtor LDCs by simultaneously writing off loans to troubled private-sector clients and to the least solvent countries, selling loans or exchanging them for other assets (e.g., Mexican bonds), and obtaining repayments. Thus, their claims to LDCs with debt-servicing difficulties have declined by over $3 billion during that same period. As a result, the ratio of restructuring-country-loan outstandings to primary capital has been cut sharply by the money center banks from 210 percent at the end of 1982 to 110 percent as of December 1987, and probably to 100 percent as of mid-1988.

Commercial banks cannot be counted on to provide much new funding to the debtor LDCs in the foreseeable future. They may continue to provide some new money to help countries keep up with their interest payments and to cover their need for trade finance. Banks may also engage in credit operations that are partially collateralized or guaranteed. But, until the performance of the debtor countries improves significantly, banks will likely keep on attempting to reduce their overall LDC exposure relative to capital—perhaps to a level of 50 percent. Probable courses of action, even though they entail taking losses, are sales of existing loans in secondary markets to participants in debt-equity conversions and exchanges of loans for more attractive debt instruments in voluntary transactions such as Mexico's earlier this year, entailing the swap of loans for collateralized bonds.

Loan capital to support economic development over the long run is likely to be available only from official export credit agencies and multilateral organizations such as the World Bank and the regional development banks. The governments of the leading industrial countries, especially those of large surplus nations like Japan and Germany, may yet step up direct lending in support of structural reforms and private-sector expansion in the debtor LDCs. The World Bank and the regional development banks require a growing capital base to enable them to increase their loan commitments, and could well get it in the next few years. The IMF, which is the most cash-rich of the multilateral institutions, certainly should become far more generous in support of policy improvements in the debtor countries, especially in view of the sizable repayments it is receiving from them. Even so, in the best of circumstances, government agencies and multilateral organizations are likely to increase only modestly their resource transfers to the LDCs. Budgetary constraints impede major aid and lending initiatives in the key industrial countries. Moreover, even if new commitments rise visibly, net disbursements may not increase proportionately, because mounting loan repayments coming due to the development banks and the IMF are not subject to rescheduling. Thus, increased official lending will not make up for reduced net lending by commercial banks.

Reduced overall new credit inflows, combined with ongoing interest payment obligations, imply that the heavily indebted LDCs will continue to make sizable net financial transfers to their creditors. The counterpart of these net financial transfers is a real resource transfer which has averaged 4 percent of GDP since 1984 for a group of major LDCs (see Table 3).

Table 3
Resource transfers
(trade balance in goods and services, with the sign reversed)
1984-87 averages

	$ billions	As % of GDP	As % of total exports
Argentina	-2.4	-3.5	26
Brazil	-9.3	-3.7	33
Chile	-0.5	-2.7	9
Mexico	-9.5	-6.4	34
Colombia	0.0	0.0	0
Nigeria	-1.8	-3.3	18
Philippines	-1.4	-4.4	16
Venezuela	-3.3	-7.7	22
Total	-28.6	-4.2	26

Such a transfer decreases the resources available for domestic consumption and investment, making it difficult for economic growth to proceed given existing rates of savings and the current productivity level of investments.

Impatience with the lack of progress in the heavily indebted LDCs, and the prospect of continued resource transfers, have prompted proposals for wide-scale debt relief. According to debt-relief advocates, the only way these countries can hope to grow again is by ridding themselves of existing debts and related debt-servicing obligations, thereby freeing up the resources now being transferred to creditors and enabling them to borrow anew for investment purposes.

Widespread debt relief is not justified, however. The middle-income countries, such as those encompassed by the Baker initiative, are by no means insolvent. They possess considerable human and natural resources, reasonably well developed infrastructures and productive capacities, and the potential for substantial growth in output and exports—given sounder economic policies and a benign external environment. Residents of several of these countries (Argentina, Mexico, and Venezuela, in particular) have very substantial assets held abroad.

Besides, there is no assurance that debt relief would lead to better policies or an improved business climate which could trigger an outpouring of efficient investments in the heavily indebted LDCs. On the contrary, since central governments and state-run companies in the LDCs likely would be the primary beneficiaries of any debt relief, since they are the principal debtors, budgetary discipline would tend to be relaxed—possibly leading to wasteful public-sector consumption and investment spending. This would undermine the cause of reformist and entrepreneurial groups that are attempting to turn back the tide of government largesse and intervention. Moreover, debt relief would not pave the way to renewed access to private capital. Indeed, it could well result in the loss of existing access to trade credits and foreign investment, jeopardizing at the same time the potential return of flight capital.

In the end, nothing can substitute for the debtor countries helping themselves by vigorously implementing stabilization policies and basic structural reforms. These countries need to enhance the productivity of past investments, boost domestic savings while ensuring that these savings stay at home, and open up investment opportunities in areas that will yield exportable production. Attention likewise needs to be focused on how best to attract at least a portion of the assets held abroad by the residents of the debtor countries, as well as how to induce greater foreign direct investment. In these ways they can achieve satisfactory growth while still transferring some resources to creditors, thereby restoring credit-worthiness.

The Role of Foreign Direct Investment

It should be stated from the outset that foreign investment inflows cannot be expected to grow in the near term to the point where they will compensate for the loss of access to large-scale bank lending for debtor countries. For a group of major debtor LDCs, these inflows amounted to $6.8 billion last year, up from an annual average of $3.9 billion during 1984-86 and above a 1979-81 average of $5.7 billion (see Table 4). These figures are quite modest in comparison with the $26 billion per annum that these countries were able to obtain from foreign commercial banks, on average, during the heyday period 1979-81. On the other hand, capital inflows of the magnitude seen in the late 1970s and early 1980s are unlikely to be seen again—and were clearly unsustainable.

Furthermore, the importance of foreign investment is not captured by these commonly cited statistics. To begin with, multinational companies in any given country command far more investment resources than the flow of funds from parent to affiliate companies would suggest. For example, U.S. Commerce Department data show that, during the six-year period from 1981 to 1986, U.S. investment flows to Latin America totaled a mere $1.9 billion, but that capital outlays by affiliates during that time in fact were nearly $24 billion (see Table 5). The reason is that a varying, but in recent years overwhelming, proportion of capital expenditures on the part of multinational companies operating in the debtor LDCs has been funded by internally generated cash flows and resources borrowed locally, rather than financing from abroad. This is understandable considering the massive devaluations and tightened exchange controls witnessed in most countries since the outbreak of the debt crisis. These developments have discouraged local affiliates from increasing their foreign-currency-denominated liabilities to back the acquisition of local-currency-denominated assets.

Table 4
Foreign direct investment inflows
$ billions

	Average 1979-81	Average 1984-86	1987, of which			
			Total	Cash	Con-versions	Rein-vestments
Argentina	0.6	0.6	0.6	0.1	0.0	0.5
Brazil	2.3	1.1	1.0	0.2	0.3	0.5
Chile	0.3	0.2	0.9	0.2	0.7	n.a.
Colombia	0.2	0.8	0.3	0.2	0.0	0.1
Mexico	2.0	0.6	3.2	1.1	1.5	0.7
Nigeria	0.0	0.3	0.4	0.4*	0.0	n.a.
Philippines	0.2	0.1	0.3	0.1	0.2	0.0
Venezuela	0.1	0.1	0.1	0.1*	0.0	n.a.
Total	5.7	3.8	6.8	2.4	2.7	1.8

*Includes reinvested earnings

Table 5
U.S. foreign direct investment and U.S. affiliates' capital expenditures in Latin America*
$ billions

	Investment	Capital expenditures
1981	2.7	5.3
1982	1.4	5.0
1983	-2.0	3.3
1984	0.4	3.3
1985	-0.9	3.6
1986	0.3	3.2
Cumulative total	1.9	23.7

*Excluding banks. Also, Panama and the
Caribbean are not included

In addition, foreign investment is arriving increasingly in a form—debt-to-equity conversions—capable of improving the structure of the debtor countries' external liabilities and of reducing the total amount of these liabilities and associated payments. As can be seen in Table 6, the external liabilities of the major LDCs are not only very large, but are disproportionally concentrated in foreign debt rather than equity. This lopsided structure is undesirable: debt service obligations are a function of fluctuations in the foreign currency in which the debt is denominated and in the applicable international interest rate— factors beyond the control of borrowing countries and bearing no relation to the use to which borrowed funds are put. Equity service obligations, on the other hand, are determined by the fate of productive investments: profit and dividend remittances are made when there are gains to be distributed—reflecting directly the degree of success of business ventures and, indirectly, the country's economic performance and political climate. There is a clear need to restructure external liabilities in these developing countries away from overdependence on foreign debt and toward reliance on equity.

Table 6
Stock of external liabilities
$ billions, estimates as of year end-1987

	Foreign debt	Foreign investment	Total	Foreign debt as % of total
Argentina	55.0	9.6	64.6	85.1
Brazil	121.3	28.9	150.2	80.8
Chile	21.3	3.5	24.8	85.9
Colombia	17.1	5.0	22.1	77.4
Mexico	105.7	19.9	125.6	84.2
Nigeria	26.0	4.8	30.8	84.4
Philippines	30.5	2.4	32.9	92.7
Venezuela	36.4	7.5	43.9	82.9
Total	413.3	81.6	494.9	83.5

Conversions of debt into equity are ideally suited to achieve this restructuring because they do not add to a country's total external liabilities; on the contrary, they usually subtract. These conversions entail the purchase—in the secondary market for LDC debt—of a foreign-currency obligation of a private- or public-sector entity, swapping it for cash or a liability of the same obligor that is denominated in local currency, and then using the cash (or selling that liability in the local financial market to raise cash) to make an equity investment. If all of these transactions were carried out at par and at no cost, the stock of the country's external liabilities would be unchanged, since the increase in foreign investment would equal the decrease in foreign debt. The worthwhile objective of raising the capitalization and diminishing the overindebtedness of a developing country would be achieved.

But, in fact, LDC debt can be purchased for a very substantial discount, and a portion of it is normally shared with the private- or public-sector entity that is redeeming the obligation or with the government that authorizes the swap. In the case of Chile, for example, the government imposes no tax on a transaction between a foreign direct investor and a local debtor. In practice, however, the purchaser of the debt can persuade the issuer to redeem it only if it is willing to share the discount in the secondary market—by accepting a smaller amount of cash or a local-currency liability of lesser amount. In most of the other major debtor countries, the authorities impose a conversion fee based either on an auction of conversion rights (Argentina and Brazil) or on the desirability of the investment being contemplated (Mexico and the Philippines). These fees drive a wedge between the amount of the original (foreign-currency) and the new (local-currency) obligation. In reality, therefore, the conversion of debt into equity results in the most desirable of outcomes—namely, in a restructuring and reduction of external liabilities, with this reduction leading to a consequently lower level of service payments.

Debt-to-equity conversions obviously appeal to foreign investors, who thereby lay out less of their home currency or end up with more local currency than they could otherwise. This cuts the start-up costs of whatever business venture they intend to launch. Some observers regard this as unfortunate; in their mind, conversion programs bestow an unnecessary "subsidy" to foreigners who are willing to invest anyway. But this is a very narrow view of debt-to-equity conversions. To begin with, the country grants no subsidy at all; the only participant in the conversion process that underwrites everyone else's gain is the original creditor bank that is willing to accept a cash price below par for surrendering the claim on the debtor LDC. Second, the fact that conversions result in lower start-up costs across the board may well entice foreign investors to undertake ventures that they would not otherwise have launched, or to undertake them sooner or on a larger scale.

The most important contribution that foreign direct investment can make to the heavily indebted LDCs, however, is to play a catalytic role for improved resource utilization. Multinational corporations are generally the best positioned to start utilizing domestic resources effectively, bring down production costs, incorporate modern technology, and develop new markets in order to facilitate export-oriented economic growth. Their managers are accustomed to the competitive environments found in industrial countries, where the ability to adapt quickly to changed circumstances is expected. They can transfer technology directly from their parent companies and use it or sell it through licensing, franchising, marketing, turnkey, or services contracts. They have access to information and markets to enable them to gauge demand abroad for goods and services. To unleash the creative energy of foreign investors, however, existing obstacles will need to be removed.

Obstacles to Foreign Direct Investment

Foreign investors in most developing countries have been subject to discriminatory treatment. Multinational companies have been effectively barred altogether from entering certain fields (e.g., financial intermediation, media), from holding a majority ownership, or from bidding for government contracts, and they have been told which is the lowest acceptable level of local content in production, what minimum portion of sales shall be devoted to overseas markets, how technology may be transferred from parent companies, and to what extent they may borrow funds domestically. These targeted regulatory practices have narrowed the interest of foreigner investors to business opportunities carrying few risks and promising the highest profits, and they have reduced the flexibility of multinational corporations to mix labor, capital, and technology in the most efficient manner.

Beyond adverse discriminatory treatment, foreign investment has been discouraged by the usually obstructive, arbitrary, and unpredictable character of the general body of business regulations and economic policies in most developing countries. Price controls or freezes are imposed suddenly and then relaxed abruptly. Taxes are often imposed or abolished by decree, even in the more democratic regimes. Imports and exports of particular items can be banned in response to temporary gluts or shortages. Currencies are prone to large devaluations, or else to being fixed at uncompetitive levels for long periods of time. Uncertainty brought about by regulatory and policy changes has discouraged domestic and foreign investment alike, and these regulatory and policy swings many times have sealed the fate of business ventures.

Two additional deterrents to foreign—and local—investment have arisen in recent years in heavily indebted LDCs. One is heightened uncertainty associated with transition to more representative forms of government, whether in Latin America or in the Philippines. The new democracies have sought to revise laws and practices put into place by dictatorial regimes in the 1960s and 1970s and, in so doing, have opened protracted debates of private property rights and the participation of foreign capital. The most lamentable case is that of Brazil, where the drafting of a new constitution, already over a year in the making, has greatly upset the business climate. Besides incorporating principles costly to all companies operating there, the new text apparently will admit foreign investment "only and exclusively" in the national interest, and will enshrine discriminatory treatment of multinational companies by making the distinction between truly national companies (defined as those headquartered in Brazil and whose controlling shareholders shall be "permanently, exclusively, and unconditionally" Brazilian) and the rest. Companies that are truly Brazilian will be entitled, for instance, to prospect for "strategic" minerals; the others will not.

Recession or slow economic growth since the onset of foreign debt difficulties, often combined with high and erratic inflation, constitute the other major recent deterrent to foreign as well as local investment in heavily indebted LDCs. Consumer spending has had to be cut sharply to reduce trade deficits, stem capital flight, and rebuild foreign exchange reserves. GDP per capita declined by 7 percent between 1981 and 1987 in the major debtor LDCs (see Table 7). Corporate performance deteriorated and foreign companies suffered accordingly: in the same group of major debtor LDCs, profits were 20 percent lower during the four-year period 1983-86 than during 1979-82. Inflation—and largely ineffective attempts to curb it—have heightened uncertainty and hindered operations. Moreover, the shortage of foreign exchange led to the imposition of exchange controls in most countries and to tighter restrictions on earnings remittances. In Argentina, for example, cash remittances have not been authorized, and multinational companies have instead received dollar bonds (BONEX) that they have had to sell at a discount to investors in that country to obtain dollars; in Brazil, Mexico, and other countries, foreign exchange for remittance purposes has been subject to delays of many months; and in the remainder, foreign investors wanting to remit have had to do so at unfavorable exchange rates.

Table 7
Real GDP per capita
1981 =100

	1982	1985	1986	1987
Argentina	93	90	93	93
Brazil	99	103	109	110
Chile	84	87	90	94
Colombia	99	101	104	108
Mexico	97	91	86	86
Nigeria	94	79	74	72
Philippines	99	83	84	87
Venezuela	98	84	86	86
Total	95	91	93	93

Recent Initiatives

The paucity of net new financing for debt-burdened LDCs, whether from commercial banks or official institutions, has increased awareness in government circles of both industrial and developing countries of the desirability of an enhanced role for foreign direct investment. U.S. Treasury Secretary Baker was among the first officials to acknowledge, in the October 1985 statement that has become known as the Baker Initiative, the desirability of such an enhanced role. This awareness has been followed by some worthwhile multilateral and unilateral initiatives in the past couple of years.

On the multilateral front there is the establishment of the Multilateral Investment Guarantee Agency, or MIGA, which finally became effective in mid-April of this year. This World Bank-affiliated agency will guarantee eligible foreign investments against losses resulting from noncommercial risks such as expropriation, civil unrest, and restrictions on currency transfers. In addition, it will carry out research and promotional activities, increasing the flow of information and expertise related to the investment process in developing countries. As of April, twenty developing and nine industrial countries had formally accepted membership, with over thirty others indicating their intention to join in the near future. Of the countries with debt-servicing difficulties, Chile, Ecuador, Jamaica, and Nigeria are among the twenty which have subscribed to MIGA, and the Philippines among those that have stated they would.

One significant regional effort to promote greater foreign investment is the agreement of the Andean Pact countries (Bolivia, Colombia, Ecuador, Peru, and Venezuela), in early 1987, to increase their autonomy in member country dealings with investors and to modify the most restrictive aspects of their infamous Decision 24. Even before that agreement, Ecuador and Venezuela had liberalized their treatment of foreign investors; Venezuela, in particular, had greatly reduced the authority of a government agency (SIEX) that had been a thorn on the side of foreign investment. In July of last year, following the agreement, Colombia raised the ceiling on profit remittances and authorized foreign firms to gain access to the Andean market without phasing down to majority local ownership.

Chile and Mexico provide examples of recent unilateral action to welcome foreign investment. Chile has had a very open regime toward multinational companies since 1974. In 1985 it amended its legislation to make it even simpler and more appealing to foreign investors, while putting in place the most liberal—and therefore the most active—debt-to-equity conversion program in existence. The country's foreign investment law is simple and among the few that is based on the principle of non-discrimination between foreign and local investors. Mexico, for its part, has been showing greater flexibility in interpreting foreign investment legislation by approving, for instance, full foreign ownership of companies in key high-technology areas. Its in-bond industries are proving more and more popular and its debt-to-equity conversion program, now suspended—temporarily, it is hoped—generated a great deal of interest in the investor community.

The availability of guarantees, more favorable legislation, and a positive attitude toward foreign investment, certainly are necessary elements to stimulate the arrival of multinational companies in the heavily indebted LDCs. However, the element that is still missing in most countries is a radically improved business climate—new investment opportunities arising from deregulation and privatization in the context of relatively predictable economic policies and political stability.

Among the debt-burdened LDCs, only Chile has gone very far in this direction, although, admittedly, its favorable business climate could yet be affected by the coming transition from a dictatorial to a more democratic regime. In recent years Chile has vastly improved the performance of government-owned companies, many of which were deficit-ridden, and is now engaged in a sweeping privatization program. The country's previously very weak banking system has been strengthened, and equity and securities markets have been deregulated, to the point where Chile boasts the most competitive, efficient capital markets in Latin America. The government has stuck to a relatively liberal foreign trade and payments regime, despite debt-servicing difficulties; it is succeeding in diversifying exports and substituting imports, without subsidies or import restrictions. The authorities have worked in conjunction with foreign bank creditors, the World Bank, and the IMF, obtaining advice and as much financial support as possible under the circumstances.

Overall investment, and foreign investment in particular, is increasing vigorously in Chile—regardless of the looming political transition and the country's small size and distance from overseas markets. Capital formation has increased steadily from a low of 10 percent of GDP in 1983 to 16 percent last year, and may well rise to 18 percent of GDP this year, for one of the strongest recuperations witnessed among the heavily indebted LDCs. Foreign investment has risen from a low point of under $70 million in 1983 to over $600 million last year and a projected $1 billion in 1988, mostly via debt-to-equity conversions. Moreover, the investment that is taking place in Chile is in areas of competitive advantage—in natural resources and manufacturing for export. The reason is that in Chile the prices for most goods and services are set competitively because markets for commodities, labor, and capital are not distorted by government intervention or protectionism.

Mexico is a good candidate to attract sizable foreign investment in the near future if the business climate there continues to improve. Significant progress has been made in the area of trade liberalization and public-sector rationalization. In the past three years, Mexico has moved from a very closed import system and an overvalued currency to an open regime with few quantitative barriers, low tariffs, and a competitive exchange rate. This has lowered the cost structure of industry and enabled it to increase sales abroad. Exports other than oil reached $12 billion last year, or 58 percent of total exports, up from $5.3 billion in 1982, the equivalent to one-quarter of all exports. Public-sector rationalization, meanwhile, is being achieved through the privatization, liquidation, or merger of state-owned companies, as well as through increased operational efficiency in enterprises remaining in government hands. However, the incoming administration of President Carlos Salinas needs to consolidate the reform effort by deregulating the economy and bringing inflation down permanently. If it accomplishes this, the business climate in Mexico will prove to be very attractive for foreign direct investment.

It is in such a context that foreign investment can best realize its promise—to contribute to economic growth by mixing the resources available locally with imported technology, management, and marketing know-how. It is also the context necessary to spur productive investment on the part of residents, and the one needed to attract the flight capital to help fund the economic recovery of the debt-burdened developing countries.

V. Protecting Foreign Direct Investment: An International Law Perspective

By Detlev F. Vagts

Introduction

As states of the developing world modify their stance vis-à-vis foreign direct investment (FDI) and seek to attract rather than repel that force, they turn to consider how to diminish investors' perception of country risk. This paper addresses the various means through which a state can attempt to diminish that risk or, more precisely put, how it can diminish the risk as perceived by potential investors.

One should, right at the outset, acknowledge that legal rules and instruments can play only a limited role in fostering that sense of security and, beyond that, in stimulating the flow of investment. A sense of security is the product of a national environment and of its history; legal assurances can only bolster a sense of stability generated by that history. At the broadest, one observes that it is the hope of making a profit, of finding valuable minerals or a moderately paid and highly efficient work force or a significant market of reasonably affluent consumers that motivates a corporation to make a move into a country. The risk of adverse government action is merely a set-off against that positive figure, and absence of risk is not by itself an affirmative attraction.

It is most convenient to approach the government's task of diminishing the perception of risk by looking at the reasonably well elaborated theory that guides potential investors, accustomed to evaluating an investment in terms of its estimated future earnings or cash flow. More technically, this theory is as follows: The planner would take the estimated return year by year on the investment made. The return for future years would be discounted to its present value by applying an appropriate rate of return. Thus if, starting with the second year of the project, it is expected to return $100 each year, the value of the second year might be discounted by 10 percent to $90, the third year to $80, etc. The annual returns added together produce the expected return of the project. That value is then compared with the rates expected from the other investments open to the calculating entity. Naturally, it is impossible to predict just how the investment will turn out; it is more feasible to plot several paths that the future may take. One can assign a probability and an expected value to each such turn of events and then calculate the yield on that option. One's expectations then can be worked out as the sum of the expected values times their likelihood of occurrence. To put it simply, if one implies three equally likely outcomes to an oil drilling venture—a total dry hole, a gusher and a trickling mediocrity—one can say that the possible outcomes are: 1/3 times $0, 1/3 times $1000 and 1/3 times $100 or a total of $366 2/3.

Political risk comes in at this point. One needs to calculate the possibility and the effect of an outcome in which the oil well is a gusher but the government takes it away and does not pay for it. Thus one assigns an N percent chance of a confiscation and a dollar value to that confiscation. One bears in mind the fact that the loss may not take place until years of successful operation, so that its present value remains fairly high even after the heavily discounted deduction. One also notes that few expropriations have resulted in a 100 percent loss, since most expropriators pay something, even if it is only a fraction of the investment and is delayed for a long period of negotiating and arbitrating.

A full calculation of these risks includes the possibility of adverse governmental actions not amounting to expropriation. A government may increase taxes 50 percent, impose new wage requirements, intensify pollution control or plant safety regulations, etc. There may be interruptions owing to riots or civil insurrection. Exchange controls or moratoria may be imposed. While the effect of these may not be as catastrophic as an outright expropriation, the probability of their happening may be a good deal greater so that the negative value they subtract from the total expected returns may be large. In a country such as the United States, one may feel no concern about expropriation without just compensation, but one cannot regard the risk of higher taxation or stiffer regulation as of no account.

Having established a schema for these calculations, one scrambles around for numbers to plug in. There is no scientific discipline for predicting adverse government interventions. There are some sources that make a living by providing believable guesses about the

103

"political climate" of foreign countries. Decisions are, in fact, made upon the basis of educated guesses about risk, often without any particular assignment of numbers. (But note that if an investor chooses to take a plunge in profitable but risky country Y rather than stable but commercially disadvantaged country X there is an implicit judgment that the risk value was greater than the commercial advantage of Y over X, which may have been quantified with some precision.) Similarly, a decision to enter the market of X is an implicit calculation that the political risk of Y is more than its business advantages over X.

It is this process, intuitive and somewhat irrational at times, that states seeking foreign investment try to influence. They should be aware that executives who make these decisions are often excessively influenced by acquaintances who have strong views about a country's stability but who may be ill-informed, biased or temperamentally unsuited to gauging risk. Thus a national policy to reduce perceived risk is, in a sense, tilting at phantoms. Much of it belongs in the fields of public relations and advertising. Yet an intelligently conceived legal policy can influence the calculations. Lawyers do play an important role in investors' evaluation processes — more in some countries than in others and more in some enterprises than others, to be sure. While a good lawyer will be realistic enough not to take the written word for the reality of security, legal assurances are the beginning of the trail.

We turn then to a consideration of the different ways in which a state can provide legal assurances of stability and security to foreign investors. They involve different levels of enactment as well as different types of subject matter. Some of them can be done by the state on its own, others require joining with other actors.

Unilateral Assurances

A state can give assurances to foreign investors simply by telling them specified policies will be followed. It is common to publish brochures and other advertisements that mingle handsome photographs of the nation's scenery and its diligent work force with assurances of the country's welcome. In point of fact these seldom have significant legal effect although it is conceivable that they could later disable the country from making various arguments to international tribunals in defense of measures taken against foreign investment. In any case, it is a start.

The next step is to embody those assurances in legal documents such as regulations or statutes. This makes the possibility of the state's reversing course more remote and change harder to affect. But it is at the heart of the concept of a sovereign state that it can change its mind and issue new regulations or amend and supersede previous legislation. The idea that one regime cannot bind its successors is common to a wide range of legal systems. What can be done to "entrench" such rules? Nothing much unless the state is so organized that some set of rules—such as its basic law or constitution—has priority over others. In such a system, a basic norm can be dug in that forbids excessively retroactive changes in law (e.g., the U.S. contracts clause) or the taking of property without due compensation (e.g., the U.S. Fifth Amendment or the French Declaration of the Rights of Man). The core meanings of such documents sink into the national consciousness. After nearly 200 years of living with proclamations of the inviolability of property, American and French peoples take for granted the no-taking-without-paying idea. That is not to say, however, that both legal systems have not accumulated substantial experience with disputes over when the legitimate exercise of regulatory functions shades over into a forbidden taking without compensation, or what is meant by due compensation when the object taken has unique qualities. In a state where there is little industry and little case law on business issues, a guarantee that the state will grant the alien investor all the safeguards, rights and privileges that accrue to nationals has little concrete meaning. If there is no locally-owned mining industry, the state's law of mining enterprises can be changed without inhibition by the thought that the treatment given the foreign miner is different from that afforded natives.

The factor that gives all of these provisions of law real meaning, i.e., meaning that allows lawyers to give comforting advice to prospective investors, is the institutional underpinning. Specifically, this implies some institution that can interpret the fundamental law—and win respect for and compliance with its rulings.

Lawyers in capital-exporting countries will tend to measure institutions elsewhere against the ones they know at home. The U.S. Supreme Court, the French conseil constitutionnel, the Bundesverfassungsgericht and the high courts of other countries stand as examples. Lawyers are prone to judge the judicial institutions of unfamiliar countries rather harshly and assume chauvinistically that only their system can provide real justice. Still, it is possible for courts to build up a reputation for consistency and even-handedness through their work in both routine and exceptional cases.

Possession of such a judiciary is a major plus in establishing a favorable foreign investment climate. Need one add that it has advantages for the regular citizenry as well? Those advantages can be lost, and frighteningly quickly, if a revolution comes and tosses all of these institutions into the dustbin of history, substituting for them drumhead courts-martial or specially stacked administrative tribunals. Establishing such general tribunals is such a long and difficult task that some states may prefer to establish special ad hoc solutions for disputes with foreign investors.

Contractual Assurances

Instead of acting in its capacity as legislator, a state may choose to deal with the foreign investor in its capacity as contractor. Particularly if the planned investment is a unique one, it may seem simpler to write a contract tailored to a specific enterprise rather than enact generalized legislation. There may be a hope that the contract will be more binding than legislation that responds inevitably to changes in the sovereign's will. These agreements are not easy to draft but developing countries are becoming more sophisticated about writing them and about finding expert help and advice from outside sources, either international organizations or national professionals.

What would be the contents of such an agreement? We have a fair-sized, though quite incomplete, array of such agreements, some of them published, some collected and filed by international agencies. Of course, particular attention has been paid to mineral exploitation agreements, once known as concession agreements and more recently as development agreements. In outline, such an agreement would cover the following issues:

First, it would define what is granted to the company by way of exploration and extraction rights; the extent in space and the duration in time of the rights would be specified. One observes that the typical term of such agreements has shrunk over the years. Where sixty-year terms were once common, experience has shown that human foresight will not reach that far into the future and that events will not stay stable for so long.

Another part of the agreement will spell out what the company agrees to do. Some of this is physical—the areas the company will explore for minerals, its obligation to do so in certain ways and at a specified pace, then its obligations with respect to refining and extracting the minerals it finds. Some of it is financial—the company is to pay specified sums in return for its rights. Some of this may be a downpayment, some may be a flat periodic payment, and some may be designated as royalties or taxes and be measured either by a percentage of the gross value of the output or of the net earnings.

Other provisions will allocate to the parties functions as to the provision of infrastructure such as roads, hospitals and the supply of water and electricity. In the case of a manufacturing enterprise, it is likely that the provisions will be less elaborate and that, in particular, the obligations of the investor as to the management of the plant will not be spelled out but entrusted to the discretion and profit-motivation of the entrepreneur. In fact, the agreement may relate only to the special benefits which the government is providing, with some modest provisions as to the entrepreneur's contribution—perhaps its commitment to invest specified sums in the operation.

A critical element of such contracts is the clause relating to the settlement of disputes. It might refer issues arising under the arrangement to the host country's regular courts, or to its special courts that deal with government contracts, or to a specially established body outside that system. The outcome depends on the host's bargaining position and its sensitivity to the issue. Both in the United States and in civil law countries it is common for government contract cases to be shunted into special channels and dealt with by such bodies as the Court of Claims, the Board of Contract Appeals, or the conseil d'état. Where no reliable and predictable tribunal exists ready to hand, with the personnel and the track record to inspire confidence on the part of outsiders, the parties may decide to create a special and unique forum.

Some states strongly resist any such suggestion that their tribunals be bypassed. Self-confident industrial states ignore the whole idea. States in Latin America, remembering the 19th century experience with arbitral tribunals imposed by European and American pressures, tend to adhere to the Calvo clause by which foreigners seeking admission to the country's economy agree to forego appeals to diplomatic or other international remedies. Those legal remedies which are enough for the citizenry of the state are adequate for foreigners as well.

On the other hand, a number of states in Africa, the Middle East and the Far East have acceded to requests by foreign investors for arbitration clauses that put issues between investors and states outside of the jurisdiction of the regular tribunals. Drafting such a clause is a matter of some complexity. In a sense, all of the issues about the constitution and procedures of the arbitral tribunal must be specified because the operation lies outside of the regular national legal system. In fact there are ready-made institutional arrangements that can be "plugged into" the contract between the investor and the state. One can, for example, specify that procedural matters shall be governed by the rules developed by the United Nations Centre on International Trade Law; in that case the UNCITRAL rules are supposed to guide the arbitrators at their work. If one specifies that the International Chamber of Commerce system is to govern, one gets more guidance. The ICC has a procedure for naming the arbitrator or arbitrators, for deciding where the hearings are to take place, what the costs are to be, etc. In any case, a decision must be reached as to whether there is to be a single arbitrator or several (usually including party-appointed arbitrators) and what sort of limitations as to neutrality and legal standing are to govern the selection of arbitrators.

A difficult question is that of the designation of the substantive law which the arbitrators are to apply. One might, in ordinary commercial matters, expect that the law of the place principally connected with the transaction would be made to govern. That would presumably be the law of the state where the investment is being made. But that gets one back into types of problems we have previously reviewed. The arbitral tribunal will be powerless to decide in favor of the alien, whatever may have been its rights at the time the contract was signed, if the sovereign contractor changes its law. Thus, drafters seek to "freeze" the law pertaining to the contract.

Prominent among the ways in which this is attempted is a clause mandating that the arbitrators decide issues under the contract by referring to some law outside the host country. This law would remain unchanged (it is assumed) despite the best efforts of the host's lawmaking machinery. One could choose the law of the investor's home country or that of some wholly neutral state that possesses a sufficiently advanced and detailed legal system to offer answers for the questions that are likely to arise. Reference to a foreign system is apt to seem offensive to the host state, even if its own legal system is too primitive to provide materials to solve modern commercial or industrial problems.

What else is there? Drafters have tried to fashion a reference that would be neither that of the host country nor of any other. Much has been written about internationalizing a contract, that is, making it subject to international law. The theoreticians object that in its essential character, international law is the law that governs relations between states (and, secondarily, international organizations). They would say that the parties cannot, by providing otherwise, make international law apply to a contract that is not a treaty between states. More practical writers object that international law does not contain answers to the major questions likely to arise in dealings with foreign investors.

The standard sources of international law do not answer questions that have arisen in the cases, such as: what is a workmanlike way of financing and operating a hotel in Djakarta, or what are the rights of Saudi Arabia, in shipping oil out of the country, to choose a contractor other than Aramco, the party with whom the state contracted as to exploring for and extracting the minerals. Some would say that what these clauses really tell the arbitrators to do is to examine the civil/commercial law systems of the leading jurisdictions and deduce from them those commercial law concepts that are common to all.[1] While difficult questions are in fact likely to receive somewhat divergent answers from the major legal systems, this does give arbitrators something to work with as they struggle towards a solution. It is in a way rather like the law of merchants or lex mercatoria, which some writers see as being revived nowadays through the efforts of commercial arbitrators. Those who draft such a clause should recognize that there is a great deal of flexibility within such a directive and that the character and origin of the arbitrator(s) who decide the specific issues is going to have a good deal of influence on the outcome.

In fact, most internationalization clauses are a mixture. Typically they would have local (Saudi Arabian or Libyan) law govern except where in conflict with international law which, it is provided, would prevail in that case. The principles of international law in question presumably are the idea of pacta sunt servanda and the rule against uncompensated expropriations. This may be backed up by an explicit "freeze" of various local laws and regulations. These versions leave considerable room for the operation of local rules that are not confiscatory or in breach of terms of the agreement.

---

[1] In effect this is a "general principles" idea under Article 38-1(c) of the Statute of the International Court of Justice rather than "international conventions" or "international custom" under Article 38-1(a) or (b).

If a dispute in fact goes before such an arbitral tribunal and the investor is successful in convincing the panel of the rightness of its case and in obtaining an award, what then? What does the investor really have? Looking at the record of cases one comes away with quite a positive impression. Eventually, after considerable commotion and maneuvering in foreign courts and in the petroleum markets, Libya's Qadaffi did pay the oil companies whose contracts he had flamboyantly cancelled. Other oil states in the Middle East have likewise done what arbitrators ordered. Only a few scattered episodes of persistent failure to honor an award to a private party mar this record.

If one looks at the legal situation, the picture is more complex and shaded. When the host country is a party to the 1958 United Nations Convention on the Recognition and Enforcement of Foreign Arbitral Awards, the award is, by treaty, entitled to recognition in both the host state and any other state that is a party to the Convention. This embraces nearly all of the states of the industrialized world and a wide sampling of the remainder. That commitment may require the other state to permit the attachment and execution of the host state's property found within its territory. That would depend, however, on the degree to which the enforcing state would permit execution on a foreign sovereign's property with respect to its own judicial orders. Thus, in the United States a foreign arbitral award against a state would be enforced on property in this country only to the extent that it was commercial, and not diplomatic or military property. Other questions might arise, such as the extent to which property held in the name of a state instrumentality that had no connection with the dispute that gave rise to the award could be attached. Other states are not likely to be more generous than the United States. In any case, a creditor with an award in its favor is considerably better off than one who is simply trying to enforce a cause of action based on expropriation or breach of contract in foreign tribunals. Such a party is likely to encounter objections based on the act of state doctrine or similar rules in other jurisdictions—which should have no place in the enforcement of an arbitral award. One observes that even such claimants, notably Kennecott Copper in relation to Chile, have had considerable success in interfering with the export trade of the expropriating state. With an award, a corporation ought to have even more leverage. [1]

---

[1] We postpone to the section on multilateral arrangements the possibility of inserting a clause in the contract that refers the matter to the International

Bilateral State-to-State Agreements

One way to try to reassure potential investors is to enter into an agreement with the investors' home governments in which the host state makes commitments with respect to the investment. For a long time these were generally included in what were termed treaties of friendship, commerce and navigation, or conventions of establishment. As they grew out of the nineteenth century, these constituted a medley of commercial matters. They might contain clauses as to the powers and duties of consuls, tariffs, access to ports, etc. As relates to our subject matter they characteristically included clauses dealing with protection against expropriation, with access to courts and general national treatment provisions.

By the time the United States had gone through a modernization program in the 1950s, it had quite a network of such agreements. However, they included primarily states of the industrialized world (other than Great Britain) which, as matters of internal law, generally afforded aliens the rights spelled out in the treaties. There was resistance on the part of developing states that tended to see the agreements as one-sided in effect. Treaties with Ethiopia and Iran, concluded while they were governed by strong conservative monarchies, did however contain protective provisions. One of them became significant in litigation in American courts between the Ethiopian government and the Kalamazoo Spice Corporation that ended with an intergovernmental settlement. The other has played a significant role in the decisions of the Iran-United States Claims Tribunal at the Hague, obviating the need to prove that the requirement of compensation in the event of a taking was an established rule of customary international law. On the other hand, the unexpected use of an old treaty by Nicaragua in its litigation against the United States over the latter's support of the contras has undoubtedly cooled the enthusiasm of the State Department for general treaties of friendship, commerce and navigation, especially when, like Nicaragua's, they contain clauses that submit disputes arising under them to third-party adjudication.

Centre for the Settlement of Investment Disputes, which gives the investor additional assurances with respect to dispute resolution.

In the last two decades, a new form of bilateral treaty has been gaining popularity. That is the bilateral investment treaty or "BIT." These agreements could be referred to as stripped-down friendship commerce and navigation treaties. They can be quite short in format, dealing only with protection of investment and covering such issues as contract termination and compensation for expropriation. Some of them are involved with quite a few issues, thus constituting a real package of investment arrangements. While their contents vary widely, they often include sweeping—but somewhat vague—assurances of national treatment, most-favored-nation treatment and fair and equitable treatment of foreign investment. This may extend to tax questions. Somewhat tighter provisions may deal with the right to have foreign employees enter the country and work there, with competition between the foreign enterprise and state-controlled entities and with the right to repatriate earnings on invested funds, even during periods of foreign exchange stringency.

Various European states, particularly Switzerland, were pioneers in the use of this approach. The United States was a latecomer and as of this moment the agreements which the United States has signed are still awaiting Senate consent. At a time when there are several hundred pairs of such treaties it is curious that we have not progressed further in providing that additional assurance for our enterprises.

So far, as the literature discloses, BITs have not yet been put to the test so that we do not really know how much they enhance the security of foreign investment. Most of them have been between states that are on good terms with each other and so it is perhaps not surprising that, in the climate of recent years, litigation has not arisen. A priori it would seem that such an agreement, with a clause providing for resort to the International Court of Justice or an ad hoc international tribunal, would be comforting to the investor. One does have the suspicion that specific investor-host contracts would be better at addressing the specific problems that worry that particular investor.

Another type of agreement that can be called bilateral is the agreement between the host government and the investor's home government that relates to an arrangement under which the home government insures the investment. Consider the United States investment guaranty program, now managed by the semi-governmental Overseas Private Investment Corporation. Typically OPIC insures the American investor against expropriation loss, inconvertibility of currency or war, riot and insurrection (or against all three). It charges an insurance premium for this coverage which is specified in an elaborate agreement that had been developed over the years by OPIC and its predecessors. As part of this program OPIC seeks assurance from the host country as to its rights over against that country in the event that the investor is able to make its case against OPIC either through negotiation or through the arbitration provided by statute and spelled out in the guaranty contract. This is termed a right of subrogation, in the vocabulary of insurance firms. OPIC made claims before the Iran-United States claims tribunal in cases where it had paid off insured investors. Since it puts the resources of a large insurance firm—and ultimately the full faith and credit of the United States—behind an investment, this type of insurance should have a powerful comforting capacity. One notes, however, that the program is limited in a substantial number of ways by the authorizing legislation. Thus it is the U.S. Congress and not the host country that determines the availability of insurance coverage. Also, it is not without a price, since the insurance premium is not insignificant and will have to be recovered by the investor if the enterprise is to produce a full net profit as expected. Moreover, the coverage will likely not reimburse the investor to the full extent of the losses of expected gains as distinguished from the original investment.

Multilateral International Arrangements

Various mechanisms operating at the multilateral level between states are in operation or proposed, in an effort to alleviate concerns about investment security. First and foremost we have the International Convention on the Settlement of Investment Disputes. ICSID is designed to provide a neutral forum to which parties can submit a dispute arising under an investment agreement. In order for an agreement to get to that forum it is not sufficient that the state be a party to the Convention. It is also necessary that it give its consent to such adjudication either by including such a commitment in its legislation on foreign investment or by spelling it out in a contract with the investor. While a large number of states are parties to that agreement, Latin American nations have in general been reluctant to accede to it, presumably out of traditional concerns that led to the Calvo Clause; and some states that are parties rarely, if ever, make it applicable. Still, since its inception, ICSID has received a total of 23 cases, of which 5 have actually been decided by its arbitrators.

Two recent cases in which awards in favor of the investor were annuled by an appeals process within ICSID have led to articles by investor-oriented lawyers expressing concern about the reliability of the institution as a bulwark for investors. Of course, representatives of host governments will reply that it is not the function of ICSID to produce an award for the foreign investor in every case but to serve as an impartial adjudicator who will occasionally find that the state was not in the wrong.

A proposal that is currently before the nations of the world for their accession is that of the Multilateral Investment Guarantee Agency, also a World Bank proposal. This agency, if it receives the stipulated number of ratifications by states from both the capital exporting and capital-importing world, will serve on a multinational basis the same needs now being serviced by national insurance agencies in the industrialized world. Although it does not in its text contain commitments by the states parties not to expropriate property or repudiate contracts, it would inhibit such actions. For one thing, it contemplates that MIGA will obtain commitments from states in which investments are made that are comparable to those the states give to national insuring agencies. It is too early to tell how well MIGA will fill gaps in the existing availability of guaranty coverage and how well it will assure investors.

What about a multinational commitment as to the substance of investor protection, i.e., a promise not to take without paying or not to repudiate contracts without cause? In the 1950s some distinguished European lawyers proposed a draft multilateral convention to give such generalized assurance. It met with cool response from the developing countries and has not been heard from for some time.

There was a series of resolutions by the United Nations General Assembly that were promoted as providing assurances and clarifying the rules of customary international law. The 1962 resolution was hailed by industrial countries as meeting their needs for security, although it was interpreted variously by different states who read somewhat ambiguous language about compensation as reflecting their views. Ambiguity was perhaps inevitable in a document that gained such a wide consensus among capitalist, socialist, industrialized and developing states. It was followed in 1974 by another resolution, the Charter of Economic Rights and Duties of States, which seemed to read out of the field any commitment to a supranational standard of compensation, leaving it to the state doing the taking to decide what it could and would afford. This was at the height of the euphoria among developing countries that followed the oil crisis of 1973 and its demonstration of the power of the oil producing states. Now that neither the oil producers nor other suppliers of raw materials have cause to feel very powerful perhaps a majority of the UN General Assembly could be persuaded to back a resolution that would be at least as affirmative at that of 1962.

Conclusions

A state seeking to reassure foreign investors has various alternatives that I have outlined above. Of these, the most suitable and least wasteful seem to be tailor-made specific agreements with investors or with investors' home countries. These allow for a maximum of flexibility and attention to the particular needs and desires of particular investors, or at least investors from a particular country. A tightly drafted development agreement can deal with each one of the investor's concerns about expropriation or lesser adverse governmental actions. If it is the status of labor regulation or environmental rules that worries the foreigner, for example, those can be addressed in highly specific detail without encumbering the state in actions on other fronts.

Internal constitutional commitments seem too cumbersome and burdensome to make for the sake of a foreign investor alone. They should be taken on only if they correspond to the nation's own internal vision of itself.

Going the route of multinational arrangements may be too cumbersome in a different sense, that of involving too many different national actors with conflicting interests. They also tend to deprive a state of the means of differentiating itself from all the other states. If property is secure everywhere, the country with particular guarantees loses its edge.

In working towards security for foreign investment, a state should not lose sight of certain cautions. The present state of the world economy, and in particular the dire straits of much of the developing world, should not cause states to go too far in making concessions. History shows an incessant cycle of changes. A nation that surrenders too much of its control in 1990 may regret it by 2000. Each commitment should be looked at realistically. If useful, expert advice should be gotten from an outside source, private or governmental. The investor

115

should be made aware how special some of the concessions are. They should be limited in time so that they do not project their effects too far into a remote future where the configurations of forces and effects are very different.

Foreign capital should get its quid pro quo and no more. History is full of examples of states that squandered their inheritance in profligate dealings with foreign finance that left another generation to pay a heavy price. Those who direct the foreign economic policy of developing states in this difficult period should learn from their history.

Bibliographical Note

Since this is a normative rather than analytical and technical piece and is addressed primarily to non-lawyers I have not encumbered it with detailed footnoting I would otherwise provide. In lieu thereof I offer this brief bibliographical note as a guide to sources that might be helpful in pursuing any particular interest.

On investment decisions in general consult any basic treatise on corporate investment such as R. Brealy & S. Myers, Principles of Corporate Finance (2d ed. 1984). Those principles were applied to the expropriation of foreign investment sphere by Hu, "Compensation in Expropriation: A Preliminary Economic Analysis," 20 *Virginia Journal of International Law* 61 (1979). I collected references to risk analysis in international investment in "Foreign Investment Risk Reconsidered: The View from the 1980s," 2 *ICSID Review* 1 (1987).

The rules on general international law protection of foreign investment are set forth in *Restatement, Third, Foreign Relations Law of the United States* § 712 (1987). For a critique of that section arguing that it understates the protection given under international law, see Clagett & Poneman, "The Treatment of Economic Injury to Aliens," 22 *International Lawyer* 35 (1988). For questions about what acts constitute expropriation, see Dolzer, "Indirect Expropriation of Alien Property," 1 *ICSID Review* 41 (1986); questions about the risks of unfavorable changes in law within the U.S. are treated in Kaplow, "An Economic Analysis of Legal Transitions," 99 *Harvard Law Review* 511 (1986).

On treaties of friendship, commerce and navigation see R. Wilson, "United States Commercial Treaties and International Law" (1960) and Walter, "Modern Treaties of Friendship, Commerce and Navigation," 42 *Michigan Law Review* 805 (1958). On bilateral investment treaties see Gann, "The U.S. Bilateral Investment Treaty Program," 21 *Stanford Journal of International Law* 373 (1985).

On the drafting of development agreements see D. Smith & L. Wells, *Negotiating Third World Mineral Agreements* (1975) and as to arbitration clauses Dubisson, "La négociation d'une clause de règlement des litiges," 7 *Droit et pratique du commerce international* 77 (1981). The outcomes of some recent important arbitrations under such clauses are discussed in von Mehren & Kourides, "International Arbitrations between States and Foreign Private Parties: The Libyan Nationalization Cases," 75 *American Journal of International Law* 476

(1981). See also Lalive, "Contrats entre états ou entreprises étatiques et personnes privées; Développements récents," 181 *Receuil des cours* 9 (1983); Delaume, "State Contracts and Transnational Arbitration," 75 *American Journal of International Law* 784 (1981); W. Peter, *Arbitration and Renegotiation of International Investment Agreements* (1986).

On investment insurance or guarantee arrangements see T. Meron, *Investment Insurance in International Law* (1976) and OECD, *Investing in Developing Countries* (5th ed. 1983).

On the proposed multilateral agency see Shihata, "Towards a Greater Depoliticization of Investment Disputes: The Roles of ICSID and MIGA," 1 *ICSID Review* 1 (1986).

VI. A PROGRAM LEADING TO AN INTERNATIONAL AGREEMENT ON FOREIGN DIRECT INVESTMENT

By D. L. Guertin

Introduction

In the past two decades the world of international investment has changed dramatically. The level of foreign direct investment (FDI), has increased from $115 billion in 1967 to several hundred billion dollars in the late 1980s. More significantly, the number of home countries having a significant stake in the treatment of foreign direct investment by host countries has grown. For example, in 1967 Japanese FDI was $1.5 billion. By the early 1980s it had increased to about $40 billion. In 1960 FDI by developing countries was less than $1 billion. It had increased to $18 billion by 1981. FDI by developing countries includes significant investments in developed as well as developing countries. Examples include the purchase of the Andover Oil Co. in the United States by the Kuwait Petroleum Corporation in 1982 and the Marine Midland Bank, Inc. by the Hong Kong and Shanghai Banking Corporation in 1980.[1]

As levels of FDI and the number of countries having a stake in such investment have increased, bilateral and intergovernmental efforts to promote and protect this investment and to guide the relationships between international investors and host countries have also multiplied. Since the late 1960s, more than 300 bilateral investment

---

[1]Sources of information on foreign direct investment include:
International Investment and Multinational Enterprises: Recent Trends in International Direct Investment. Organization for Economic Cooperation and Development (1987). Table III 7.
International Direct Investment: Global Trends and the U.S. Role. U.S. Department of Commerce (1984). Table I.
International Direct Investment: Global Trends and the U.S. Role. U.S. Department of Commerce (1984).

treaties (BITs) have been signed. These treaties have laid down principles for the promotion and protection of FDI.

A number of intergovernmental organizations—in particular the Organization for Economic Cooperation and Development, the UN Centre on Transnational Corporations, and the World Bank—have also worked extensively in this area. The World Bank, for example, now has three affiliates working on FDI: two placing particular stress on promotion,[1] including in one case investment insurance, and one organization functioning effectively in arbitration of investment disputes.[2]

These increased levels of investment and intergovernmental activities on FDI have occurred, in many instances, despite adverse rhetoric about foreign direct investors in the 1970s. The level of rhetoric has greatly decreased in the 1980s. There is widespread recognition of the benefits of FDI and increased confidence on the part of host countries that they are capable of effectively managing their relations with the foreign investor.

The late 1980s therefore provide four essential ingredients for reviving work on an international investment agreement. They include: an increased number of host countries having a more significant stake in such an agreement; a more positive attitude toward FDI by many home countries; a body of agreements (in particular BITs) on FDI; and an institution which could serve as an acceptable forum in which to develop an international investment agreement, viz., the World Bank.

This chapter proposes a work program that would culminate in an international agreement on FDI, to be negotiated under World Bank auspices. The chapter will first review the significance of the hundreds of BITs that have been negotiated in laying the foundation for such an agreement. It will then outline an international program of work which could culminate, in 10 to 15 years, in a World Bank Declaration on International Investment.

Bilateral Investment Treaties

Following unsuccessful efforts to develop international investment agreements as part of the aborted International Trade Organization

---

[1]The International Finance Corporation (IFC) and the Multilateral Investment Guarantee Agency (MIGA).
[2]The International Centre for the Settlement of Investment Disputes (ICSID).

after World War II and again in the Organization for Economic Cooperation and Development in the 1960s, a number of European governments undertook programs to develop bilateral investment treaties. These effort have resulted in over 300 BITs,[1] mainly between European governments and developing countries. The United States was late in undertaking a BIT program, launching its efforts in the early 1980s. The United States has now signed and ratified eight treaties. As will be discussed below, the hundreds of existing treaties have laid a sound foundation of principles for broader intergovernmental understandings on investment promotion and protection.

Investment Issues Treated in Bilateral Investment Treaties

Bilateral investment treaties have been designed to cover several issues of interest to the investor: treatment of the investor after an investment has been made in a host country; expropriation, compensation and transfer of funds; and dispute settlement.

It is well recognized that many other governmental policies are critical to investors; for example, macro-economic policy, taxation, price controls, protection of intellectual property, and performance requirements. While BITs in a few instances address the latter two subjects, other intergovernmental approaches are used to influence policies in the other three areas enumerated. The World Bank and the IMF, for example, are making great efforts to encourage governments to adopt sound macro-economic policies that are supportive of market mechanisms and the private sector.

The sections of a typical treaty are noted below:

I.   Definitions
- investments covered
- geographic areas covered

II.   General Statement Regarding Promotion and Protection of Investment

III.   Treatment of the Investor
- does not include right of establishment
- generally includes fair and equitable treatment, most-favored-nation treatment

---

[1]UN Centre on Transnational Corporations, *Transnational Corporations in World Development: Third Survey* (1983). *Fourth Survey* (1988).

IV. Expropriation
- in the public interest
- for a public purpose
V. Compensation
- should be prompt, adequate and effective
- some statement on how compensation should be determined
VI. Transfer of Funds
- provides that compensation can be effectively transferred
VII. Exceptions
- deals with exceptions in cases of customs unions or instances in which other international agreements cover an issue (e.g. tax treaties)
VIII. Dispute Settlement Between Investor and Host Country
IX. Dispute Settlement Between Host and Home Countries
X. Government Assumption of Investors Claim if a Government Makes a Payment to Investors

A Profile of Bilateral Investment Treaties

More than 300 BITs have been signed between developing and developed countries. As noted previously, they cover treatment, expropriation, compensation, transfer of funds and dispute settlement. A paper presented at the 1982 Montreal Conference of the International Law Association (ILA) provides an excellent overview of the countries participating in BIT treaties and the types of protection provided by the treaties.[1]

Most of the BITs in the ILA listing have been signed between European governments (158 out of 173) and either Asian (46) or African countries (102). See Table I for details. Table II outlines in some detail the provisions of 50 BITs with developing countries (LDCs).

---

[1] *Permanent Sovereignty, Foreign Investment and State Practice.* (Report for the ILA International Committee on Legal Aspects of a New International Economic Order). Peters, Paul, Schrijver, Nico, J., and deWaart, Paul J.I.M., (1982).

Treatment of Investor

These treaties, as noted in Table II, do provide for fair and equitable treatment. The language on national treatment provides for treatment no worse than that given to nationals, in about half of the treaties analyzed. These treaties do not include references to international law in the treatment section. Such a reference would help assure that governments would treat foreign investors as well as domestic investors, or in line with international law, whichever is more favorable.

Expropriation, Compensation, and Transfer of Funds

The expropriation sections of these treaties generally state that expropriation should be in the public interest or for a public purpose. About two-thirds of the treaties provide for non-discriminatory treatment and due process of law.

The compensation section of these treaties universally recognize that compensation is required. Nearly all treaties provide that compensation should be prompt and effective (transferable).

Table I:
Geographic Distribution of Bilateral
Investment Treaties
(OECD ex U.S. with LDCs, ex Centrally Planned Economies)

DC	# of BITs	Africa	Asia	Latin America	Middle East
Bene-Lux	10	5	5	-	-
France	22	11	6	3	2
FRG	48	29	10	5	4
Italy	4	4	-	-	-
Japan	7	2	3	2	-
Netherlands	15	10	5	-	-
Sweden	7	5	-	2	-
Switzerland	33	23	5	3	2
U.K.	19	7	8	1	3
Other	8	6	-	2	-
	173	102	42	18	11

Peters, Paul, et al, Permanent Sovereignty, Foreign Investment and State Practice, Report for the ILA International Committee on Legal Aspects of a New International Economic Order.

123

Table   2

Provisions of 50 Foreign BITs With LDC's

Paul Peters - Montreal Conference.

International Law Association - 1982

Subject	% Covering
Standards of Treatment	
Fair and equitable	88
Security and protection to investments	72
No impairment of basic rights of investor (management)	64
MFN Treatment	88
National Treatment - shall not be worse than to	52
own nationals	
- In some cases does not apply to admission	
- Others make provision for exceptions to	
national treatment	
Expropriation and Compensation	
Conditions for expropriation	
- In public interest or for public purpose	92
- Non-discrimination	66
- Due process of law	62
- Compensation required	100
Compensation	
- Fair, equitable or adequate	16
- Detailed treatment, such as "normal (Transferable)	80
and "return,"..."without reduction in value due to	
...seizure..."	
- Interest until date of payment	12
- Compensation fixed before expropriation	62
- Compensation should be effective (Transferable)	96
- Prompt or without (undue) delay	98
Arbitration	
- Provision for arbitration	100
- Time limit for exhaustion of local remedies	24
- Mandatory ICSID arbitration at the request of	Large majority
the investor	
- Provision for inter-state arbitration	100
- Direct access by investor to arbitration procedure	38
(Germany & Switzerland do not use ICSID)	

Subject	% Covering
International Law	
- Specific reference to international law (generally on expropriation and compensation)	52
Termination of Treaty	
- Protection after Treaty terminated	96

Dispute Settlement

Arbitration of disputes is covered in all of these treaties. A large majority require mandatory arbitration by the International Center for the Settlement of Investment disputes (ICSID) at the investor's request. The dispute settlement procedure is, however, weakened as only about a quarter of the treaties provide for a time limit on the use of national efforts to resolve a dispute before moving to international arbitration. In addition, the investor only has direct access to the arbitration procedure in about 40 percent of these treaties. This, then requires the investor to work through its national government.

Sensitivities in the Treatment Sections of Bilateral Investment Treaties

The treatment section of bilateral investment treaties is especially sensitive for host country governments.[1] Ideally this section would provide for right of establishment (initial investment in a country) and national treatment for investments once they are established.

Some of the treaties signed in the late 1960s did approach this standard; for example, the Malaysia treaty with the Federal Republic of Germany. (See appendix A).

By 1979, when Malaysia signed a treaty with Sweden, the Bumaputra program designed to give preferential treatment to the indigenous Malay population was in place, and foreign investors were to be given treatment no less favorable than that accorded to investments by nationals or companies of third states. In other words,

---

[1]Bilateral investment treaty dates noted in text. Full texts of treaties are available in ICSID publications "Investment Treaties."

most-favored-nation treatment was granted, but not national treatment. (See Appendix A.)

Article 2.2 of this treaty addresses the earlier granting of national treatment in, for example, the treaty with the FRG, stating that more favorable treatment can be given to companies of other states if granted by an earlier treaty.

Some treaties signed by Singapore further illustrate the sensitivities in this area (Appendix B). In the 1972 Singapore-Netherlands Treaty, Article VII.2 provides for national treatment, but with no reference to international law. By 1975 another treaty (Singapore-UK), while providing for treatment for foreign investors no less favorable than that given to nationals (Sections 3(1) and 3(2)), added a provision 3(3) providing for less favorable treatment if "its (Singapore's) laws so provide in respect of all non-nationals and in relation to particular matters."

In some cases, the language in this section of a treaty is even more general than the examples above and basically provides for fair and equitable treatment as well as most-favored-nation treatment.

While the treatment sections of the BITs are generally the weakest sections of these treaties, it is important to recognize that the BITs provide as much or more protection than a 1967 OECD Draft Convention on the Protection of Foreign Property[1] (Appendix C).

Bilateral Treaties With the PRC

It is worthwhile commenting on the BITs negotiated between the People's Republic of China (PRC) and a number of countries for several reasons: there is continuing interest in investing in the PRC; the PRC has demonstrated far more interest in such treaties than any other centrally planned economy; and the PRC treaties effectively illustrate a number of difficulties in negotiating such treaties.

Standards of Treatment

The seven PRC treaties[2] reviewed in Appendix D generally provide for fair and equitable treatment as well as most favored nation (MFN)

---

[1]For a discussion of the OECD Draft Convention on the Protection of Foreign Property see G.W. Haight, 2 *International Lawyer* (1968), 326-353.

[2]Treaties reviewed: Belgium-Luxembourg, Federal Republic of Germany, France, Italy, Netherlands, Norway, Romania.

treatment. As would be expected, there are no international law references in this section. The principle of national treatment is to a large extent useless to a foreign investor in the PRC, as the investor expects better treatment than that provided for national enterprises.

Standards for Expropriation and Compensation

As will be seen in the accompanying appendix, standards for expropriation and compensation should be satisfactory to most investors. There is provision for expropriation to be in the public interest, non-discriminatory and under due process of law.

Compensation is to be without unreasonable delay, convertible, and freely transferable. While the terms prompt, adequate, and effective are not used, this language is helpful.

The treaty language regarding the amount of compensation is not completely satisfactory. For example, the treaty between the People's Republic of China and West Germany (FRG) refers to compensation amounting to the value before expropriation, with no definition of value.

Standards for Transfer

Given the PRC's chronic shortage of foreign exchange, it is to be expected that this section of the treaties would be of minimum assistance to the foreign investor. For example, the PRC/FRG treaty, which is representative, provides for:

> ...a guarantee of unrestricted transfer of current and capital transactions without undue delay, using funds in the investors' foreign currency account and in accordance with foreign exchange regulations; in exceptional circumstances, China shall make available foreign currency for capital to maintain or increase investment, royalties, loan payments, returns and liquidation proceeds; rate of exchange based on IMF cross rate.

Dispute Settlement

The dispute settlement provisions of these treaties all provide for binding state-to-state arbitration of disputes. Some of the treaties provide that decisions of an arbitral tribunal shall be based on generally recognized principles of international law adopted by the governments involved. The treaties generally provide for arbitration between the investor and the PRC government only on the amount of compensation.

Future Role of BITs

The existence of more than 300 BITs is invaluable in demonstrating the interest of LDCs in attracting investment and, more importantly, in demonstrating that most LDC governments recognize a number of responsibilities to the foreign direct investor.

Bilateral investment treaties should continue to play a vital role, as they are:

(1) widely accepted;
(2) specifically designed to address key fundamental investment issues;
(3) contributory to the development of useful international law standards;
(4) flexible enough to be adopted to meet the varying needs of a range of host and home countries (example: adaptation to the Bumaputra program in Malaysia);
(5) used to establish rules of the game for investment between developing countries (examples: Egypt-Kuwait treaty signed in 1965; Iraq-Kuwait treaty signed in 1964).

The Role of Intergovernmental Institutions

As valuable as BITs can be, it is essential that governments recognize the need and the timeliness of mounting significant efforts in the remainder of this century to develop an international agreement on investment. This will require a great deal of political will by many governments because of some continuing sensitivities regarding foreign investment. Given the growing impracticality of isolating national economies from each other, and the obvious linkages and in some cases substitutions of investment for trade, it is not enough to have an international trade regime, the GATT, without a counterpart for investment.

In my judgment, it will not be possible for the GATT, given its already rich agenda, to address investment issues—except perhaps those immediately related to trade—in the coming decade.

It is therefore necessary to turn to other institutions, preferably those with some investment experience coupled with high acceptance by both foreign direct investors and governments. Two institutions satisfy this requirement in my view: the World Bank and the Organization for Economic Cooperation and Development (OECD). The UN Centre on Transnational Corporations, while having made many worthwhile contributions in the field, is not as broadly accepted by key nations having international investment capabilities as either the Bank or the OECD.

The OECD

Because of its leadership role in intergovernmental work on investment, as exemplified by the OECD Declaration on International Investment and Multinational Enterprises, it is essential that OECD members play significant roles in any international investment programs. In addition to their roles as individual governments, the OECD as an institution can and should participate in strengthening international investment agreements. It should begin by strengthening the existing OECD agreement on national treatment and then develop a revised OECD Declaration. The revised Declaration would bring together agreements by OECD governments designed to promote and protect international investment.

The proposal developing such a revision of the 1976 OECD Declaration on International Investment and Multinational Enterprises is presented in a forthcoming paper.[1] In brief, the revised OECD Declaration would include: voluntary guidelines for multinational enterprises; a convention bringing together existing OECD understandings on right of establishment, national treatment, expropriation, compensation in line with international law standards, free transfer of funds, and dispute settlement; a reaffirmation of governmental commitment to the use of ICSID for resolving investment disputes between an investor and a government; and a decision to consult on investment incentives and disincentives.

The completion of a strengthened OECD Declaration is important for several reasons:

---

[1]*Building an International Investment Accord.* Guertin, Donald L. and Kline, John M., forthcoming.

1) It will demonstrate the continuing commitment of OECD governments to sound international investment principles by bringing together in one document existing OECD understandings of investment.
2) It will serve as a guide for subsequent negotiations on an international investment agreement under World Bank auspices.
3) It would cover about 70 percent of existing international investment and future inter-OECD investment.

The World Bank

The World Bank has been active in the investment policy area since 1956. The Bank now has three agencies working in this field: the International Finance Corporation, the International Centre for the Settlement of Investment Disputes, and the Multinational Investment Guarantee Agency.

The International Finance Corporation

The International Finance Corporation (IFC), which is affiliated with the World Bank, began operations in 1956.[1] Its key objective is to promote economic development in Third World countries through support of the private sector. The IFC provides private business with equity and loans without government guarantees. The IFC, therefore, acts as a catalyst to foster private investment when other sources of capital are not available. The organization also provides technical assistance and recently has begun to offer advice on policies and institutions that should be established to attract and regulate foreign investment.

The investment promotion activities of the IFC include an advisory service on policies and institutions that can assist members in attracting and regulating foreign investment. The advisory service program will assist developing countries in formulating:

- general strategies toward foreign direct investors
- policies to attract investment in specific sectors
- strategies to promote foreign investment

---

[1] For additional background see Foreign Investment Advisory Service, available from IFC.

- policies on technology transfer
- ways of increasing the effectiveness of government institutions dealing with foreign investors.

Other investment promotion strategies of the IFC include:

- identification of firms in developed countries that are interested in developing country investments
- identification of investment opportunities in developing countries
- direct marketing to increase business awareness of IFC programs
- development and promotion of investment opportunities
- development of "new financial products and services that will meet the needs of industrial country investors."

The International Centre for Settlement of Investment Disputes

Another World Bank affiliate, the International Centre for the Settlement of Investment Disputes (ICSID), was created in 1965. The organization was established to assist in the conciliation and arbitration of investment disputes between member states and nationals of other member states.

Ninety-seven states have signed and eighty-nine states have ratified the Convention establishing ICSID (June 30, 1987). They include twenty-two OECD governments, Canada and Spain being notable exceptions. While some Caribbean governments have signed and ratified the Convention, no South American governments are signatories. A number of Asian and African states have also signed.

Since its founding, twenty-three cases have been submitted to the Centre, fourteen of which have arisen since 1981.[1] This indicates a growing interest in the use of ICSID. As noted earlier, the 1982 ILA paper on BITs states that a large majority of BITs have sections covering mandatory ICSID arbitration at the request of the investor. More specific information on cases is presented in "ICSID Cases, 1972-1987," available from ICSID.

There are certain prerequisites for submitting a case to ICSID.[2] A dispute must be between a contracting state and a national of another

---

[1] *4 News from ICSID* (Winter 1987), and ICSID Cases, 1972-1987.
[2] Taken from ICSID, Document ICSID/12.

contracting state. The parties must agree to ICSID conciliation or arbitration through a clause in an investment agreement or by agreeing to submit an existing dispute to the Centre. Agreement to settle the dispute cannot be unilaterally withdrawn. The dispute must be legal, not commercial. Investment is not defined and subjects such as loans and industrial property rights are included in the notion of investment.

ICSID arbitration is especially significant in that the parties are bound by the awards. Contracting states must recognize and enforce the pecuniary obligations imposed by the award as if they were a final judgment of a court of the state involved.

The Multilateral Investment Guarantee Agency

Recent World Bank efforts have led to the formation of the Multilateral Investment Guarantee Agency (MIGA).[1] This is the first time such a multilateral agency has been formed, although proposals have been discussed since the late 1940s. The great concern about the need to stimulate foreign investment in developing countries has undoubtedly been a major reason for success at this time.

MIGA has two principal roles: providing guarantees against non-commercial risks; and working to improve investment conditions and promoting investment in developing countries. The latter role can be especially significant in the long term.

The Agency was officially established in April 1988 and became operational in July 1988. Applications for investment insurance are now being accepted. Guarantees for individual projects are expected to be $50 to $70 million. In April 1988, 63 countries had signed and 31 countries had ratified the agreement. These 31 countries account for 54 percent of MIGA's authorized capital of $1.1 billion.

The guarantee program covers four types of non-commercial risk:

1)   restrictions on currency conversion and transfer
2)   expropriation, including creeping expropriation (actions by governments which, in effect, deprive the foreign investor of ownership or control)

---

[1] J. Voss, "The Multilateral Investment Guarantee Agency: Status, Mandate, Concept, Features, Implications," *Journal of World Trade Law*, August 1987. "MIGA's Technical Programs for the Encouragement of Foreign Investment." Background Paper for Consideration of Chapter Six of the Draft Operational Regulations (1986).

3) breach of contract in cases where a foreign investor has no access or lacks timely access to a judicial hearing or arbitration
4) armed conflict or civil disturbance

These programs, while extremely desirable, do not directly address the policies and practices of governments for the promotion and protection of foreign investors.

MIGA will undertake several programs aimed at improving the Third World investment climate for foreign investors. These programs will provide consultation and advise on policies to encourage direct investment.

MIGA will provide the following assistance to host countries desiring assistance in attracting foreign direct investment:

- research
- dissemination of information on investment opportunities and the climate for investment in host countries
- technical assistance, when requested by members, regarding investment, promotion and policies to attend foreign investment
- policy guidance and advice regarding investment agreements relating to MIGA's role as a guarantor of an investment.

Over time, MIGA's activities should contribute to the development of an international consensus on the fair treatment of foreign direct investment. This work should also address the policies of home country governments regarding outward investments.

Initial emphasis in these activities will, however, be directed towards supporting the guarantee programs of the Agency.

As described earlier, the World Bank, the International Finance Corporation and the International Centre for the Settlement of Investment Disputes all play roles in fostering constructive policies for the promotion and protection of investment. The need to coordinate these activities and avoid duplication is specifically covered in MIGA's Operational Regulations which state:

"The Agency shall cooperate with, rather than duplicate, the work of other agencies of established competence in the economic and financial aspects of national environments for foreign investments."

Given its broad role and limited resources, it will be some time before the Agency can mount a fully effective program to promote and protect FDI.

133

While initial coordination with other Bank affiliates—IFC and ICSID—should proceed smoothly given their different areas of emphasis, coordination may become more difficult as the range of policy and technical support roles of these affiliates broadens. In a few years, therefore, it may be desirable to review the investment related activities of the Bank affiliates (IFC, ICSID, and MIGA) to determine if a more formal coordination mechanism or restructuring may be desirable.[1]

A World Bank Declaration on International Investment and Multinational Enterprises

The more than 300 BITs provide a sound foundation for developing a broader intergovernmental agreement designed to promote and protect FDI in both developed and developing countries.

Rather than create a new institution, it would be preferable to use an existing institution, the World Bank, to develop such an agreement.

The Bank has several advantages over other intergovernmental institutions in undertaking such an activity:

1) It is better accepted by both developed and developing countries than other institutions.
2) Its role includes work on macro-economic policies as well as investment policy. Sound macro-economic policies are critical in establishing a good climate for investment.
3) The Bank has worked on investment policy questions since 1956.
4) A key Bank affiliate (ICSID) has a record of dispute resolution through *binding* arbitration.
5) Another affiliate (MIGA) furnishes additional opportunities for work on investment policy and provides for an investment insurance program.
6) The Bank has had extensive experience in the evaluation of major investment projects. The Bank's energy program, for example, had an annual budget of about 3 billion dollars at its highest point, in the mid 1980s.

---

[1]The IFC and MIGA have established a joint venture, the Foreign Investment Advisory Service, to provide advice and technical assistance to developing countries on foreign direct investment.

A World Bank Declaration would provide an instrument for bringing together in a single document principles, regarding international investment, which would be widely accepted by the year 2000 by governments of both developed and developing countries. Material presented in this paper demonstrates that there is already extensive support for a number of these principles. An outline for such a Declaration is presented in Appendix E.

In addition such a World Bank Declaration would:

- present in a single document commitments already accepted by many developing and developed country governments to international investors;
- include guidelines for international investors as well as governmental commitments;
- provide an instrument which could incorporate both voluntary and binding commitments;
- provide a base point upon which governments could build further commitments regarding international investors in the future.

The proposed Declaration's four sections are discussed below.

I.   *Introduction*

The Introduction to the Declaration would provide an outline of principles to guide governmental relations with international inves–tors. It would also recommend guidelines to international investors.

II.   *Guidelines for Multinational Enterprises*

A great deal of work has already been done on guidelines (codes) for multinational enterprises by various UN agencies and by the OECD. The OECD Guidelines for Multinational Enterprises were agreed to by the OECD Council in 1976.[1] They form part of the OECD Declaration on International Investment and Multinational Enterprises that in–cludes OECD governmental commitments to national treatment and to strengthening intergovernmental cooperation in the field of inter–national direct investment, with particular emphasis on consultation.

UN codes include the International Labor Organization's Tripartite Declaration of Principles Concerning Multinational Enterprises and Social Policy. The principles of the ILO Tripartite Declaration are the same as those used in developing the Industrial Relations Guidelines in

---

[1]Organization for Economic Cooperation and Development, *International Investment and Multinational Enterprises*, revised edition 1984.

the OECD Guidelines for Multinational Enterprises. The UN Conference on Trade and Development (UNCTAD) has also developed a Code on Restrictive Business Practices.[1]

The UN Commission on Transnational Corporations has done extensive work on a code of conduct for transnational corporations that would include some material on the responsibilities of governments to these corporations. Consultation will continue on the Code, but at its April 6-15, 1988 meeting in New York, the Expanded Bureau of the Commission deferred negotiations for an indefinite time.

Given a 10-15 year time frame before a World Bank Declaration would be negotiated, at this point it is best to recognize that the guidelines in a Declaration would take into account the work noted above, along with economic and political conditions at the time the Declaration is being negotiated.

III. *Convention on International Investment*

The Convention's formulations would take into account the contents of existing bilateral investment treaties, past and concurrent work in the OECD and the UN on international investment agreements, and the extensive work of the World Bank on international investment up to and at the time of the negotiations.

The Convention would recognize the importance of international investment and reaffirm the widely held principle of fair and equitable treatment for international investors. In 10 to 15 years, when the Convention is drafted, it may be possible to include commitment to national treatment, with exceptions for purposes of national security and public order. Some limited additional exceptions may be made on an individual country basis.

A commitment to international law standards (prompt, adequate, and effective compensation), in cases of expropriation and compensation, should also be included in the Convention. Many BITs have language which, in effect, provides such commitments.

A commitment to freedom of capital movements will be difficult for some governments, given sensitivities regarding right of establishment and transfer of funds from a country having serious balance of payments problems. Such a commitment might initially address transfers provided as compensation for expropriation. The Bank, in a separate activity, should consider initiating work on codes on capital movements which could at some future date be incorporated into the Convention.

---

[1]For a discussion on guidelines and codes see: John M. Kline, *International Codes and Multinational Business.* Quorum Books, (1985).

IV. *Dispute Settlement*

Third party dispute settlement is widely accepted by many developing countries in bilateral investment treaties and through membership in ICSID.

Model BITs prepared by the Asia-African Legal Consultative Committee also have provisions for third party arbitration with references to ICSID or Conciliation Rules of the UN Commission on International Trade Law.[1] Dispute settlement mechanisms involving third parties do remain sensitive however, in particular with Latin American countries.

Such dispute settlement mechanisms are critical. As more developing countries, including those in Latin America become home countries for foreign investment, they may increasingly recognize the benefits of third party involvement.

Future Role of the World Bank

It is submitted that the World Bank, over the next 10-15 years, should become the center for work on a Declaration on International Investment. As noted earlier there are several key reasons for this view.

The Bank is respected by both developed and developing countries. It has competence in both economic policy, which is critical in laying a foundation for investment, and investment policy. It has demonstrated its ability to assist in specific investment questions relating to policy (the International Finance Corporation) and the sensitive area of dispute settlement (the International Centre for the Settlement of Investment Disputes). During the coming decade the Bank's competence and experience is expected to expand through the Investment Advisory Service of the IFC, the growing utilization of ICSISD, and the experience of MIGA.

In summary, other intergovernmental organizations having some competence in the investment area are not as widely accepted by developed and developing countries, do not provide the tie between economic and investment policy, nor do they have the extent of practical experience as the Bank.

---

[1] "Models for Bilateral Agreements on Promotion and Protection of Investments," (Unpublished manuscript) Asia-African Legal Consultative Committee.

Conclusion: An International Program for the Promotion and Protection of Investment

A worldwide program for foreign investment promotion and protection in developing countries should have the following components:

1) continuation of bilateral investment treaty programs by OECD governments with developing countries, placing increased emphasis on the roles of some LDCs as home countries;
2) encouragement of more BITs between developed and developing countries;
3) a strongly coordinated World Bank program, involving the IFC, ICSID, and MIGA, to improve the effectiveness of investment policies in LDCs;
4) completion by 1995 of a strengthened OECD Declaration on International Investment and Multinational Enterprises. Open to developing countries, this would reinforce sound principles for foreign investment policies.
5) a World Bank conference in 1995 to begin work on an international Declaration on International Investment and Multinational Enterprises.

This paper outlines such a Declaration. A sound foundation for this type of agreement has been laid by the more than 300 BITs that have been negotiated.

The World Bank, given its current and future activities in the investment area, and its acceptance by developing and developed countries is the most appropriate institution to foster such an effort.

APPENDIX A

Treatment Articles of Some Malaya Bilateral Investment Treaties

1. *Malaya-Federal Republic of Germany (1960)*

Article 2

(I) Each Contracting Party will endeavour to admit the investment by nationals or companies of the other Contracting Party in accordance with its legislation and administrative practice, and to promote such investments as far as possible.

(2) Unless specific stipulations made in the document of admission provide otherwise, investments by nationals or companies of either Contracting Party in the territory of the other Contracting Party, shall not be subjected to treatment less favourable than that accorded to investments by nationals or companies of the other Contracting Party or investments by nationals or companies of any third party on the ground that ownership, or control directly or indirectly, of them is vested in nationals or companies of the former Contracting Party.

Article 3

Unless specific stipulations made in the document of admission provide otherwise, neither Contracting Party shall subject in its territory nationals or companies of the other Contracting Party as regards their activities in connection with investments, including the effective management, use or enjoyment of such investments, to treatment less favourable than that accorded to its own nationals or companies or to nationals or companies of any third party as regards their activities in connection with investments.

Protocol:

(2) The expression "document of admission" referred to in Articles 2 and 3 shall mean a document by which a Contracting Party admits in

its territory an investment within the meaning of paragraph (1) of Article 1 to be made by a national or a company of the other Contracting Party. Such "document of admission" shall specify the favours, immunities and conditions which the former Contracting Party grants or imposes in respect of the investment admitted. Subject to the provisions of paragraph (2) of Article 2 and of Article 3, the contents of such document shall not affect the provisions of this Agreement.

(3) Article 3 shall not apply to entry, sojourn, and activity as an employee.

(4) The following restrictions shall in particular be deemed to be "treatment less favourable" referred to in Article 3: restricting the purchase of raw or auxiliary materials, of power or fuel, or of means of production or operation of any kind; impeding the marketing of products inside or outside the country, as well as any other measure having a similar effect

Measures taken for reasons of public order or security or public health or morality shall not be deemed to be "treatment less favourable" within the meaning of Article 3.

4. Malaya-Sweden (1960)

Article 2

1. Each Contracting Party shall at all times ensure fair and equitable treatment to the investments of nationals and companies of the other Contracting Party, and such treatment shall not be less favourable than that accorded to investments by nationals or companies of third States.

2. Notwithstanding the provisions of paragraph (1) of this Article, a Contracting Party, which has concluded with one or more other States an agreement regarding the formation of a customs union or a free-trade area, shall be free to grant a more favourable treatment to investments by nationals and companies of the State or States, which are also parties to the said agreement, or by nationals and companies of some of these States. A Contracting Party shall also be free to grant a more favourable treatment to investments by nationals and companies of other States, if this is stipulated under bilateral agreements concluded with such States before the date of the signature of this Agreement.

APPENDIX B

Treatment Articles of Some Singapore Bilateral Investment Treaties

1. Singapore-UK (1975)

Article 2
Promotion and Protection of Investments

(1) Each Contracting Party shall encourage and create favourable conditions for nationals or companies of the other Contracting Party to invest capital in its territory and, subject to its right to exercise powers conferred by its laws, shall admit such capital.

(2) Investments of nationals or companies of either Contracting Party shall at all times be accorded fair and equitable treatment and shall enjoy full protection and security in the territory of the other Contracting Party. Each Contracting Party shall ensure that the management, maintenance, use, enjoyment or disposal of investments in its territory of nationals or companies of the other Contracting Party is not in any way impaired by unreasonable or, except as provided for in Article 3 (3), discriminatory measures. Each Contracting Party shall observe any obligation it may have entered into with regard to investments of nationals or companies of the other Contracting Party.

Article 3
Most-favoured-nation Provisions

(1) Neither Contracting Party shall in its territory subject investments or returns of nationals or companies of the other Contracting Party to treatment less favourable than that which it accords to investments or returns of its own nationals or companies or to investments or returns of nationals or companies of any third State.

(2) Neither Contracting Party shall in its territory subject nationals or companies of the other Contracting Party, as regards their management, use, enjoyment or disposal of their investments, to treatment less favourable than that which it accords to its own nationals or companies or to nationals or companies of any third State.

141

(3) Notwithstanding the provisions of paragraphs (1) and (2) of this Article. and provided its laws so provide in respect of all non-nationals and in relation to particular matters, a Contracting Party may accord to the nationals or companies of the other Contracting Party treatment less favourable than that accorded to its own nationals or companies.

Article 7
Exceptions

The provisions in this Agreement relative to the grant of treatment not less favourable than that accorded to the nationals or companies of either Contracting Party or of any third State shall not be construed so as to oblige one Contracting Party to extend to the nationals or companies of the other the benefit of any treatment, preference or privilege which may be extended by the former Contracting Party by virtue of:

(a) the formation or extension of a customs union or a free trade area or a common external tariff area or a monetary union; or

(b) the adoption of an agreement designed to lead to the formation or extension of such a union or area within a reasonable length of time; or

(c) any international agreement or arrangement relating wholly or mainly to taxation or any domestic legislation relating wholly or mainly to taxation.

2. Singapore-Netherlands (1972)

Article II

(1) The Contracting Parties shall promote and develop economic cooperation between their respective countries.

(2) In particular they undertake to promote cooperation between their nationals and to facilitate, within the framework of their respective legislation, the participation of their nationals in the establishment of industrial and commercial activities and the provision of services in their respective countries which would contribute towards the improvement of the standard of living in and the prosperity of their countries.

Article V

Nationals of either Contracting Party shall, in the field of the protection of intellectual property, enjoy in the territory of the other Contracting Party protection not less favourable than that enjoyed by the nationals of the latter Contracting Party, without prejudice to the provisions of international conventions in the field binding on the Contracting Parties.

Article VI

Each Contracting Party undertakes to facilitate with regard to the other Contracting Party, to the extent permitted by the former Contracting Party's legislation and without prejudice to the provisions of international conventions binding on the Contracting Parties –

(a) the holding in its territory by the other Contracting Party or by is nationals of economic and commercial exhibitions and displays;

b) the importation, duty-free, of goods, materials and equipment to be used for economic and commercial exhibitions and displays, on condition that they are re-exported within a limited period;

c) the importation, duty-free, of professional equipment, and of goods, materials and equipments to be used for technical work on behalf of governmental bodies or private enterprises on condition that they are re-exported within a limited period;

d) the re-exportation, duty-free, of goods, materials and equipment referred to in (b) and (c); and

(e) the disposal of goods, materials and equipment referred to in (b) and (c) in the territory where they have been used, subject to the payment of duty.

Article VII

(1) Each Contracting Party shall ensure fair and equitable treatment to the investments of nationals of the other Contracting Party and shall not impair, by unjustified or discriminatory measures, the management, maintenance, use, enjoyment or disposal thereof by those nationals.

143

(2)) More particularly, each Contracting Party shall accord to such investments the same security and protection as it accords to those of its own nationals or to those of nationals of third countries, whichever is more favourable to the investor.

APPENDIX C

Comparison of Treatment Language in OECD Draft Convention and 1968 Indonesia-FRG BIT

OECD Draft Convention - 1967

Article I—Treatment of foreign Property

(a) Each party shall at all times ensure fair and equitable treatment to the property of the nationals of the other Parties. It shall accord within its territory the most constant protection and security to such property and shall not in any way impair the management...by unreasonable or discriminatory measures. The fact that certain nationals of any State are accorded treatment more favorable than that provided for in the Convention shall not be regarded as discriminatory...

Indonesia-FRG - 1968

Section 1:4E-3.1

Except for the stipulations made in No. 6(b) of the Protocol...neither Contracting Party shall in its territory subject investments owned or controlled by nationals or companies of the other Contracting Party to treatment less favorable than it accords to investments of its own nationals or companies or to investments of nationals or companies of any third State.

APPENDIX D

Provisions of Seven PRC BITs*

Standards of Treatment	Number of Treaties Containing Provisions
Fair and equitable or similar language	6
MFN	7
International law reference	2
Expropriation and Compensation	
Conditions for expropriation	
- In public interest or for public purpose	7
- Non-discriminatory or MFN	5
- Due process of law	6
- Compensation required	7
Compensation	
- Prompt or without undue delay	7
- Transferable	7
- Based on value to investor before expropriation or real value, true value, genuine value	6
Standards for Transfer	
Without undue delay	7
Subject to PRC laws	3
In accord with foreign exchange regulations	2
China may or shall provide foreign exchange if	2(shall)
funds in investors' foreign currency account insufficient	1(may)
Dispute Settlement	
State to state binding arbitration	7
Investor-state binding arbitration on compensation	4
Reference to international law (as recognized and adopted by the parties)	3

* Belgium-Luxembourg-Federal Republic of Germany-France-Italy-Netherlands-Norway-Romania

APPENDIX E

World Bank Declaration on International Investment & Multinational Enterprises

I. Introduction
- Importance of international investment
- Recommendation of Guidelines to international investors
- Commitment to fair and equitable treatment of international investment
- Commitment to other principles such as national treatment
- Commitment to international law standards re expropriation and compensation
- Commitment to cooperation to develop agreement on freedom of capital movement
- Commitment to third party dispute settlement

II. Guidelines for Multinational Enterprises

III. Convention on International Investment
- Covering treatment, expropriation, compensation, transfer of funds and dispute settlement between governments regarding the provisions of the Convention.

IV. Dispute Settlement Between a Government and a Foreign Direct Investor

VII. FOREIGN DIRECT INVESTMENT IN THE THIRD WORLD: U.S. CORPORATIONS AND GOVERNMENT POLICY

By Cynthia Day Wallace

Introduction

Background

The Third World investment climate has changed dramatically in the past several years with the aggravation of the debt problem and the related urgency for foreign capital inflows from new sources. This situation has given rise to unprecedented efforts on the part of the developing world to attract foreign direct investment (FDI), and has indirectly led to the review of Third World investment performance requirements in the current Uruguay Round of the General Agreement on Tariffs and Trade (GATT). Other international bodies such as the World Bank and the Organization for Economic Cooperation and Development (OECD) are also reviewing various aspects of Third World investing, including not only the need to promote FDI in those countries but also the treatment of the multinational enterprises themselves in their activities abroad. The following survey was conducted to investigate and assess, from the corporate viewpoint, the most urgent aspects of this increasingly strategic issue of foreign direct investment and its implications for U.S. global economic interests.

Objective

The objective of the survey is to bring to the attention of key U.S. decisionmakers the most critical impediments currently faced by corporations investing in Third World nations, to aid in ongoing policy considerations at home, in bilateral negotiations, and in the GATT and other multilateral fora. The survey affords an opportunity to U.S. corporations to anonymously express their most pressing concerns relating to market entry, and/or ongoing operations and movements of capital, through a vehicle that can have direct policy impact.

Methodology

Corporations selected on the basis outlined below were asked what factors are considered the most (and least) critical in their investment decisions and what, if any, U.S. government actions could best alleviate their difficulties. This was done through a confidential questionnaire (Appendix A), mailed to CEOs of major multinational corporations investing in Third World countries, with assurances that all data would be so aggregated as to assure anonymity to any individual company.

Projecting a 20 percent response rate, a mailing list was compiled of some 500 major corporations investing in the lesser developed countries (LDCs). This number was attained by cross-listing the *Business Week* 1000 companies, the *Fortune* 1000, the *Forbes* magazine's annual listing of the 100 largest MNCs and a list of 500 MNCs compiled by John M. Kline of Georgetown University's School of Foreign Service for an earlier survey of firms affected by international codes and guidelines. Some omissions were allowed for internal reasons.

Participation

Time and staff limitations precluded a pre-survey "grooming" or in-depth pre-selection process that would have added more precision to the mailing. It was left to the response process itself to eliminate as non-applicable (N/A) those companies that reported no—or insignificant—Third World investments. Discounting these, as well as those companies responding that their company policy specifically precluded participation in such surveys, nearly 300 (an exact total of 295) remained. Based on the exact total, our *real participation rate equals 28.1 percent.*

With regard to size, all but two of the responding companies have annual sales of over $400 million. More than one-third of the participants are ranked in the top 100 of the *Business Week* 1000 (by "market value"), and over 50 percent are ranked among the top 200. The survey respondents include six of the ten largest MNCs on the *Business Week* 1000 listing.

149

Definitions and Clarifications

Foreign direct investment may be broadly defined as the establishment of, or acquisition of substantial ownership in, a commercial enterprise in a foreign country, or an increase in the amount of an already existing investment abroad to achieve substantial ownership. While FDI may be engaged in by individual as well as corporate investors, the present survey includes only that carried out by multinational corporations (MNCs), primarily through the establishment or expansion of a fully or substantially owned subsidiary; a merger, takeover, or other form of acquisition; or a joint venture.

Not included as FDI are other forms of international investment including portfolio investments, licensing arrangements, international holdings of official government reserves, and commercial bank lending except where loans have led to debt-equity swaps and other creative investment arrangements. Other service industries are excluded from the survey except where their activities range beyond mere trade in services to actual direct investment in or by the service company—in other words, where actual trade flows are secondary and direct investment has become the necessary agency for participation in the local market. The survey excludes all purely sales and distribution operations.

For the purposes of the questionnaire, distributed before the "graduation" of the Asian newly industrialized countries (NICs), all NICs are included within the designation "Third World."

Percentages used in the textual analysis, in the tabulated survey (Appendix A), and in the graphs (Appendices B-G), are based on the number of actual responses to each individual question, since some oral interviews did not include a factor-by-factor coverage of the questionnaire. All percentages are rounded to the nearest whole percent.

It should also be mentioned, on behalf of the corporations, that the great majority of the participating MNCs operates throughout the developing world, and the vast scope of operations of multi-industry enterprises makes it difficult to respond with precision to such a questionnaire. Large multinationals were faced with having to assess the overall importance of a given factor which might be a critical consideration for one industry and a negligible one for another. Similarly, an MNC might confront a number of factors that are critical to its operations in one region yet are nonexistent in another area of the Third World where it operates. Responses therefore represent, for the

150

most part, the composite of any given company's Third World investment experience.

Section I: Corporate Profiles and Investment Insurance

Commercial Sector

Some of the same difficulties—in terms of breaking down sector and
region—faced by the corporations responding to the questionnaire are
equally applicable to the data analysis, and for the same reasons.

The multinational corporations responding to the CSIS survey come
from a variety of sectors. Inherent in a discreet sampling is the
difficulty of examining the responses by industry. The diversification
and longevity of investment activities of some of the larger multinationals precluded assigning each company to a single sector.

Groupings by sector wherever possible, however, in an attempt to
make some industry-specific evaluations where appropriate, fall into
the following categories: financial services/insurance; health
care/consumer products/food; heavy industry; high-tech; and natural
resources. Under heavy industry is included automotive parts and
manufacture, industrial/agricultural equipment, chemicals/plastics,
and construction. The high-tech category consists of computers, electronics, aerospace, and telecommunications. The other three headings
are self-explanatory.

In all cases where one particular factor was rated critical by a large
number of companies and negligible by a significant sample of others (or
vice versa), the responses were reviewed individually to determine
whether any trends are sector-related. Again owing to multi-sectoral
and multi-regional diversification, such investigation often proved
inconclusive. The one outstanding exception is the natural resource
sector. We will return to this later on in the analysis.

The following breakdown will help to further profile the types of
companies participating in the survey: 31 percent are in heavy
industry, 30 percent in health care/consumer products/food, 25 percent
in high-tech, 20 percent in natural resources, and 5 percent in financial
services/insurance. A number of corporations fall under more than one
category, which accounts for the fact that the preceding percentages
total more than 100 percent.

In Section I of the questionnaire, each of these companies was asked
(a) to give an indication of its Third World investment position (the

151

extent and general location of its foreign direct investment in developing countries) and (b) where its investments are increasing or decreasing and the main reasons why.

Geographic Distribution

The geographic distribution of investments of participating companies covers primarily parts of Asia and Latin America. In our sampling, the Middle East plays a somewhat lesser role than the other two areas, and Africa almost none.

The reasons for a lack of interest in Africa need little elaboration. Both political risk and economic uncertainties run high in many parts of Africa, particularly sub-Saharan Africa, where the struggle for survival overrides any serious attention to sustained and healthy long-term growth.

Oil and mining companies must of course follow the dictates of natural resource availability in locating their investment facilities. One oil executive stated, "We go where the oil is." This is clearly not a decisive factor for the majority of respondents.

(1) *Areas of increasing investment*

Many of the responses received reflect a keen awareness of the growing globalization of the world economy. Of those that answered the question as to why their investments in certain regions of the developing world are *increasing*, 68 percent cited a desire to position themselves for the future. Such companies emphasized the need to gain access to potentially strategic and expanding markets in developing countries.

Asian nations such as the newly industrializing countries (now "graduated" NICs: Hong Kong, Taiwan, South Korea, Singapore), as well as Malaysia, Thailand, Indonesia, China, and India, were frequently mentioned as powerful magnets for FDI heading into the 1990s. In addition to access to new and expanding markets, several corporations highlighted the production capabilities and lower cost of manufacturing in Third World countries, especially in Asia.

While parts of Latin America, and to a lesser extent the Middle East, were also singled out as areas for increased FDI from U.S. multinationals (as with Asia, primarily for their future markets), there was some disagreement on—and a degree of uncertainty over—the prospects for FDI in these two regions. In some parts of these same regions, FDI is either increasing at a slower rate, or is actually decreasing.

(2) *Areas of decreasing investment*

Reasons cited for *decreasing* FDI in certain regions or countries are varied. Although a couple of companies expressed a reasonably optimistic view of the economic situation in the developing world, of those respondents that listed particular reasons for decreasing investment in LDCs, nearly half mentioned general economic conditions. Among the enumerated economic problems, despite claims of an "easing of the debt crisis" and "greater stability of the Mexican economy," are: "uncertain local business conditions," "devaluation of currencies," and "economic uncertainties." One executive stated simply that South Americans "just don't have money to pay for our goods."

Twenty-eight percent of those giving reasons for disinvesting specifically cited "inordinate risk" or "political instability" as causes for decreasing FDI in areas such as Central America, the Philippines, South Africa, and Argentina. An equal number pointed to changes in government policy (e.g., increasing regulation/control) as that which forced them to withdraw their investments.

Apart from the above remarks derivable from Section I responses, it remained largely impracticable—as with industrial sector identification mentioned earlier—to systematically assess specific survey data by country or region. In the rare instances in which a significant number of respondents attribute the predominance of a particular factor to a specified country or region, this correlation is cited in the text. Otherwise, any factor-specific conclusions by country or region would be highly interpretive and are thus avoided.

Investment Insurance Participation

In Section I, companies were also asked if they presently participate, or plan in the future to participate, in investment protection schemes such as the U.S. Government's Overseas Private Investment Corporation (OPIC), the World Bank's Multilateral Investment Guarantee Agency (MIGA), the International Finance Corporation's Guaranteed Return on Investment Principal (GRIP), or other such program. Only a little over a quarter of the respondent corporations are presently insured in one form or another. All but two of those companies insured are protected, at least partially, under the

153

OPIC plan. Another 8 percent are considering or planning to insure themselves under this scheme.

OPIC has served not only those companies interested in investment insurance, but also LDC governments themselves. As Clarke Ellis notes in chapter one, "LDC governments interested in improving their investment climates have consulted with OPIC about policy reforms that would help to attract investment."

Less than 4 percent of the respondent companies currently utilize the GRIP investment protection scheme. But an additional six percent are considering or planning to safeguard their investments under this arrangement. GRIP is, after all, still a relatively new insurance alternative.

The recently ratified MIGA scheme, which became operational in July 1988, has attracted the most attention and appears to be the plan with the greatest potential for the future. A significant 13 percent of the companies responding are already either considering or committed to this option. Don Guertin, in chapter six, emphasizes the dual approach of MIGA. Not only will it provide protection against non-commercial risk, but it will also work in a variety of ways to encourage FDI by improving the Third World investment climate. Guertin notes that this latter role can be especially significant in the long term.

The multinationals in the survey were also asked if they had ever participated in an insurance scheme and later withdrawn. Where this applied, the responses are quite revealing. Several indicated that they had reduced the level of investment to the point that—or initial risk had subsided to the point that—any need for insurance was eliminated. One corporation specifically emphasized the importance of comparing the cost of the protection scheme with the likely cost of a host country's instability. Another expressed a different investment philosophy which, given the fact that only 26 percent of the respondents are currently protected, may represent the practice of other of the non-insured multinationals: that they are simply not conducting operations in areas where the risk is so great as to necessitate insurance. The fundamental criterion is simply whether or not a corporation's investment is sufficiently endangered to justify the insurance costs.

In high-risk areas, or with certain high-risk operations, other forces may come into play. One company that was operating in Iran, for example, reported that when their plant was expropriated, the government-negotiated compensation settlement was greater than the OPIC benefit. Several other companies commented that insurance plans are too limited—that they are not suitable for certain industries. One international oil company, for example, suggested that these plans are "not designed for petroleum exploration type investments."

The most frequent explanation for not insuring is simply that such investment protection schemes are too costly or, more to the point, not cost effective.

Section II: Market Entry

Critical Factors

Several factors which influence market entry for foreign direct investment in LDCs are considered particularly critical by the participating companies. *Guaranteed remittance of earnings* is the factor most often rated critical (by an overwhelming 81 percent of the respondents). Not one company considers this factor negligible in its market-entry decisions. Host remittance policies reappear as the most critical cost factor as well, as we shall see in the following section.

The fact that access to hard currency earnings is critical to both the corporation and the host government creates a tension between MNC and host and heightens the sensitivity of this factor. Since foreign exchange supplies are often very low in developing countries, especially in those that are most heavily indebted, one way to safeguard the much needed inflow of foreign capital—in the face of potentially hostile public opinion—is for the host government to secure a "guarantee" that the investment will inevitably boost the foreign exchange supply. Ted Moran and Charles Pearson make this point in chapter two. The "guarantee" often takes the form of local content requirements and import/export quotas that can serve to increase costs to the multinational. The irony is, as Moran and Pearson point out, that in the very attempt to improve foreign exchange earnings by the imposition of certain performance requirements, those foreign exchange earnings may actually thereby be diminished, as potential new investments are diverted to less restrictive markets offering an international comparative advantage. Harvey Bale similarly suggests in chapter three that applying performance requirements to improve balance of payments problems has a negative impact on the expansion of foreign investment activity.

155

Interestingly enough, with the overwhelming attention accorded by our survey respondents to remittance policies and other factors related to capital movements, *exchange controls* themselves are indicated as critical to only 38 percent of the sample and *exchange rate fluctuations* is the factor rated most negligible in market entry decisions. This factor did predictably display some increased sensitivity in the "cost" and "return" sections of the survey, as we shall see later. But it is apparent that, for our respondents, restrictions on capital transfers impact Third World FDI considerably more than exchange rate volatility.

A close second and third in the ranking of most critical market-entry concerns are the *threat of war/hostilities* (critical for 77 percent of the respondents) and *protection from expropriation* (critical for 76 percent of the respondents). This is consistent with concerns revealed earlier in Section I, where 28 percent[1] of those giving reasons for disinvesting cited "inordinate risk" or "political instability" as grounds for decreasing investment in certain parts of the Third World. It is not surprising that the same concern that leads to disinvestment should be a critical consideration for initial entry into a given Third World market.

A preoccupation with political risk is particularly significant in view of the fact that nearly three quarters of the participants do not participate in investment protection schemes. Those corporations surveyed that are insured, however, do ascribe appreciably less importance to the threat of war or hostilities than do those that are not covered by some insurance program. Whereas 83 percent of non-protected companies consider this factor to be critical, the percentage drops to 58 percent for those that are insured. This means that a significant 42 percent of insured companies find the threat of war or hostilities a moderate or even negligible factor in their Third World investment decisions.

In contrast, both insured and non-insured corporations surveyed show equal caution with regard to the threat of expropriation. Regardless of

---

[1]Twenty-eight percent may not seem overwhelming in comparison with *factor-rating* percentages we have just seen, but it must be remembered that in Section I, on company profiles, the answers were *respondent-generated*. This means that over one-quarter of all respondents to the question spontaneously came up with the same grounds for disinvesting, rather than simply attributing one of three evaluations to prescribed factors, as in Sections II.A, and IV.A.

whether or not a corporation is insured, there is evidence of a desire to operate in regions where a certain degree of investment security exists. This tends to confirm the indications discussed in Section I above— including the experience related by one firm of inadequate expropriation insurance benefits—that insurance does not adequately compensate for this type of risk.

It seems somewhat surprising, with the dramatic reduction in the number of expropriations in recent years as compared with the 1970s (75-80 per year in the 1970s as against one to two a year in the late 1980s according to the UN Commission on Transnational Corporations), that expropriation is still viewed as a significant threat. This could be attributable to a cognizance that such takings decreased in proportion to the presence of foreign-owned facilities in developing countries, and that with the revival of FDI in some of the very regions where significant losses were sustained in the earlier wave of nationalizations, vulnerability is now correspondingly revived.

There is concrete reason for MNCs engaged in extractive industries in Brazil to be cautious. The 1988 revised Brazilian Constitution provides that foreigners in the mining sector will have four years to relinquish control of their assets to Brazilian nationals. The nationalization of the mining sector will impact directly on the 55 mining companies in Brazil with majority foreign ownership. These firms account for 20 percent of an estimated $3 billion in annual mineral production. Some Brazilian officials are persuaded that foreigners will adapt and find local partners, but many experts feel that Brazilian companies lack adequate capital to take over foreign interests, heightening the probability of state intervention.

The fourth most critical factor in market entry decisions is *unfavorable investment laws* of the host. Such laws are deemed a critical hindrance to market entry by 70 percent of the multinationals surveyed. Later in this section, where we analyze responses to what single U.S. government action would best facilitate market entry for FDI in LDCs, we will see an apparent disconnect between the sizable concern with unfavorable host laws and the large percentage of respondents who either explicitly or implicitly disfavor any U.S. government action to facilitate LDC investment.

Other factors mentioned with significant frequency as critical are host government *corrupt practices* (by 51 percent of the respondents) and host *barriers to imports* (by 44 percent of the respondents). Thirty-seven percent deemed the *imposition of export quotas* a critical consideration in market entry decisions, though a notable 15 percent claimed such quotas to be of negligible concern.

The generalized company profile data from Section I of the survey was used to try to determine whether any consistent industry-specific or region-specific relationship existed with regard to those corporations rating export quotas as critical in their market-entry decisions vis-a-vis those rating them as negligible. This analysis proved inconclusive, with one exception. Just under 50 percent of those companies that find the imposition of export quotas critical specifically list Mexico as at least one of the host countries for their investments, while only one of the companies that deem this factor negligible lists Mexico as a host. Beyond this single and inconclusive observation, resistance to host imposition of export quotas cannot be linked with any region or particular group of countries, nor judged to be targeted at any particular sector.

Some Observations on "Negligible" Market Entry Factors

Only 26 percent of the respondent companies are critically influenced, in their market-entry decisions, by the *availability of dispute settlement facilities*. In fact, 14 percent regard it as a *negligible* factor. It is interesting to note, however, that 81 percent of those multinationals judging this factor critical are in heavy industries such as oil, construction, industrial parts, and plastics, while only 30 percent of those judging it negligible are engaged in such industries. In an attempt to ascertain whether or not the apprehensions over dispute settlement are labor-related, a company-by-company crosscheck was made to determine if the responses to each of the two factors matched up in sensitivity.

It was found that every one of the respondent companies that deems the availability of dispute settlement facilities *critical* also considers host industrial relations policy either critically or moderately important when making investment decisions. In addition, of the 14 percent that judge the availability of arbitration facilities as a *negligible* factor, 40 percent find host industrial relations policy also of negligible importance; only one such company considers it critical. These figures, then, indicate a probable correlation between labor-related apprehensions and concerns over dispute settlement facilities.

Government Action

To the question: "What U.S. government action would be most beneficial to your company in facilitating market entry for FDI in LDCs?", the most frequent *single* response is: *more favorable tax treatment* (23 percent[1] of the companies responding to this question).

If one were, on the other hand, to *group together* all those responses that express in one way or another that U.S. government policy either has no or ought to have no real influence on MNC direct investment activities (*non-intervention/non-interference*), the result is an even slightly higher percentage (25 percent) than that for more favorable tax treatment.

Apart from specific suggestions that the U.S. government repeal existing legislation such as the Grassley Amendment[2] and the Foreign Corrupt Practices Act, and that it refrain from imposing economic sanctions, close to half of this group stated that their policies are simply not affected by the U.S. government. Nearly as many expressly stipulated non-intervention in the private sector, and the remainder simply suggested that no government action at all is needed to facilitate entry.

Interestingly, while this aggregate group of 25 percent of all respondents to the "market-entry" government-action question could be characterized as either neutral or favoring a "hands-off" policy where the U.S. government is concerned, a significant 19 percent specifically advocate government pressure or negotiation to improve certain unfavorable *host* policies.

A host country restriction may be perceived by the MNC as a problem solely with the host, with no correlation to a need for mitigating action on the part of the home government. As we saw earlier, for example, 70 percent of the MNCs surveyed rated unfavorable host investment laws as critical, yet we see here only 19 percent specifically equating alleviation of these problems with actual U.S. government action. At the same time, many might agree with a relevant note of realism sounded by one respondent, who offers the

---

[1]It is to be recalled that for the "Government Action" questions, the answers are respondent-generated, so a lower percentage carries greater weight than in the factor-rating percentages, where the factors are already furnished, simply to be rated as "critical," "moderate," or "negligible."

[2]The Grassley Amendment denies tax credits to U.S. corporations operating in countries listed in the Treasury Department's terrorism guidelines.

notion that "it is difficult to envisage how any single U.S. government action can change the mentality of sovereign nations which will effect changing means of accomplishing national (or government autocracy) objectives."

Among the suggestions mentioned for U.S. government action that rely heavily on host government response are: reciprocal treatment, easier market access, protection of intellectual property, guaranteed investment repatriation, reduced performance requirements, and more bilateral investment treaties. The last has since been given a boost by the eight BIT ratifications achieved in late 1988 by the Senate, though the United States still falls far behind the Europeans in the number of BITs concluded with LDCs. (For more on BITs, see Ellis, Bale, and Guertin, chapters one, three, and six, respectively.)

It needs to be noted here that 34 percent of total participants omitted this question altogether. If one were to make the not unrealistic assumption that no answer equates no express desire for government action, the number of "non-interventionists" would swell to a robust 50 percent of all participants. Allowing that some of this number may have refrained from responding for other reasons, such as time or sphere-of-competence constraints, each reader can draw his own conclusions. But it would be distortive not to make some reference to this detail.

While there is very little consensus, beyond tax reform and non-intervention, as to what U.S. government action would be most beneficial, a few general themes are nonetheless discernible. A significant number of respondents emphasized broad policy objectives directed at the general well-being of the international economic system. For example, one frequently mentioned item is the persistent need for a reduction in global trade barriers. Several other companies noted the importance of improving various aspects of U.S. trade policy, while a couple of others even drew in the need to balance the federal budget. While the lack of added specificity here, and the time-worn theme, lends little to the present exercise, it is of course true that balancing the budget would serve to lower interest rates, reduce taxes, and generally promote economic soundness, to the benefit not only of U.S. investors abroad but of the overall populace.

While the reduction of trade barriers is quite rightly named as benefiting FDI, it must also be remembered that such barriers can have the contrary effect, since FDI often increases in direct proportion to trade protectionism. Where such barrier reduction does spur multinational investment is of course in facilitating intra-enterprise trade transactions.

Finally, a few respondents referred explicitly to better financing terms, as well as lower U.S. interest rates. Some also urged the expansion of protection schemes to minimize risk. One participant took this opportunity to encourage the continuation of "OPIC-type" programs, and another affirmed the World Bank's MIGA as a positive move.

Section III: Cost of FDI

Critical Factors

According to the findings of the survey, the most burdensome costs associated with FDI in the less developed world stem from host government policies. The cost factor most often mentioned as critical in the investment decision process is *host government remittance policy*. Seventy-three percent of the companies participating find this factor critical, consistent with the 81 percent that consider guaranteed remittance of earnings a critical element in market entry deliberations.

Rimmer de Vries, in chapter four, suggests that those companies operating in heavily indebted developing countries are especially subject to exchange controls and tighter remittance policies. The critical hard currency shortage in these countries has led to long delays in capital repatriation (especially in Brazil and Mexico) and unfavorable exchange rates for foreign investors. De Vries describes the situation in Argentina where cash remittances have not been authorized, and MNCs must sell dollar bonds at a discount to investors in order to obtain dollars.

In a personal interview by the present writer with one executive from a major U.S. multinational, the importance of profit repatriation to the cost of ongoing investment was illustrated by his company's experience in Brazil. Under the Brazilian law regulating foreign exchange and the remittance of funds abroad, income tax due on repatriation of profits is assessed at one rate up to a certain threshold (percentage of profits), and at another rate above that threshold. The upper rate is so prohibitive that reinvestment of earnings is the only viable option, which is indeed the intent of the regulation.

For the multinational in question, reinvestment of earnings has reached saturation level. Any further expansion becomes counter-

161

productive, and the company is faced with some serious decisions, possibly to the extent of selling off some of its production facilities.

The same company is also engaged in natural resource extraction. Here the major investment incentive is, of course, the availability of the resource itself. In this aspect of its operations, the company is not dependent on the local market for its profitability, and reinvested earnings remains a viable alternative to profit repatriation.

Yet this aspect of the company's operations may be hit from another side. The revised Brazilian Constitution, promulgated in early October 1988, contains some very significant provisions aimed at those foreign MNCs operating in Brazil's natural resources sector. The document heavily favors local industry at the expense of "outsiders" and, among other new provisions, oil companies will now have to assume the financial risk for new explorations; they will no longer benefit from government subsidies.

The *natural resources* branch of the company described above suddenly finds itself faced with a fundamental change of circumstances. This situation calls to mind Detlev Vagts' observation in chapter five that constitutional amendments directed at foreign investment should be instituted only if they "correspond to the nation's own internal vision of itself." The inter-relationships are sensitive, and the "internal vision" is subject to change.

To revert to the dilemma of this same company's *manufacturing* branch, the Brazilian example outlined here—of intertwined host remittance and tax policies—illustrates how close the link can be between the two. It is not fortuitous that our survey results show these two factors in first and second place in critical impact on MNC costs. *Host government tax law and policies* was mentioned as critical by 64 percent of our sample, following host remittance policy with its 73 percent critical rating.

Close behind host government tax policies in evaluating FDI costs is *host government ownership percentage requirements* (perceived by 64 percent of our sample as critical). It is no surprise that both of these factors, impacting as they do directly on corporate profits and management control, figure among the most decisive factors in a corporation's investment strategy.

The importance of tax policies does not stop with the host government. *U.S. tax laws* are deemed critical by a solid majority of the American multinationals surveyed (again 64 percent). In fact, as a *home* country concern, tax policy far outstrips the closest contender for degree of importance in improving the lot of the corporate investor in the Third World. This will be taken up again later on in the analysis, when considering possible government action to decrease FDI costs.

Additional host-related factors judged fairly critical to the cost of FDI are *host government illicit practices* and *foreign exchange policies* (considered critical by 53 percent and 49 percent respectively). The apparent significance of host government illicit practices as a potentially critical *cost* factor to FDI is consistent with the inhibiting role corrupt practices is deemed to play in *market entry* decisions (mentioned as critical by 51 percent of the respondents in Section II). Likewise, host government exchange policies that limit capital transfers appear not only as a critical cost factor, but are, as noted earlier, a recurrent theme in each section of the survey (i.e., in "market entry," "cost of FDI," and "return on FDI").[1]

Availability and cost of raw materials and resources and availability and cost of trained labor in developing countries are also mentioned as critical cost factors by 45 and 42 percent of responding companies respectively. Forty percent of the participants also judged *host government unfair competition policies* as a critical impediment to investing in LDCs. This corresponds with current concerns over national treatment, a goal still being pursued through BITs as well as through international agreements such as the OECD Code. National treatment is named as an objective by some respondents where suggestions for U.S. government action are solicited. (See also Vagts, and Guertin: chapters six and five, respectively.)

Some Observations on "Negligible" Cost Factors

Among those cost factors considered relatively unimportant to multinationals, that most often rated "negligible" is U.S. *industrial*

---

[1]While the two foreign-exchange-related factors (exchange controls and exchange rate fluctuations) are separate under Market Entry (Section II), they are combined in the list of factors under Cost of FDI in Section III and Return on FDI in Section IV. The fact that exchange controls are rated as substantially more critical than exchange rate fluctuations in Section II, reinforced by information gathered by personal interview, would seem by extension to indicate that the "critical" responses in the other two sections (III.7 and IV.9) where the exchange rate factors together are considered critical by 38 percent and 58 percent respectively, relate more strongly to exchange controls than to exchange rate flkuctuations.

relations policies (by 36 percent). Only 7 percent of the companies surveyed consider this factor critical when making investment decisions in the developing world. Those factions of the U.S. labor force who feel that domestic job security is endangered by U.S. direct investment abroad have apparently not yet influenced U.S. policy to the point of affecting multinationals' investment decisions.

Next to U.S. labor relations policies, the *Foreign Corrupt Practices Act* is the factor second most often rated negligible (by 29 percent). It is not surprising, however, that nearly as many find it critical (25 percent). Nor is this inconsistent with the fact that over half of the respondents esteem corrupt and illicit practices *critical* in both market entry decisions and investment cost estimations. The F.C.P.A. may decrease the cost of investing by prohibiting bribes and other illicit payments by U.S. multinationals, but it also costs the MNC in terms of loss of contracts to companies of other nationalities that have not followed the U.S. model. It is no secret that U.S. companies often lose out to non-American competitors in societies where "kickbacks" and similar payments are not only acceptable, but the normal course of doing business. Many U.S. companies nonetheless still favor the law on purely moral grounds.

Of those companies that count the F.C.P.A. as a critical factor in their FDI cost calculations, 88 percent find host government illicit practices critical as well, both in considering market entry and in assessing costs after entry. It follows that those companies most concerned with foreign corruption are also most aware of the F.C.P.A. Likewise, of the companies that consider the F.C.P.A. of negligible importance in their cost-related investment decisions, a sound majority also attributes only moderate or even negligible importance to host government illicit/corrupt practices when contemplating market entry (61 percent) or when assessing FDI costs (67 percent). Obviously some of these corporations are operating in LDCs where corruption is less prevalent.

Barriers imposed on transborder data flows by host governments are deemed negligible by 27 percent of the respondents making investment decisions in the developing world. At the same time, 24 percent consider such barriers critical. As might be expected, 57 percent of those judging TBDF barriers critical are in the following sectors: computer systems, electronics, or high-tech plastics and chemicals. Only 6 percent of those responding with a "negligible" are in such industries. Seventy-two percent of those rating TBDF restrictions as "negligible" are in the following sectors: personal care, food/apparel, packaging, or natural resources. It stands to reason that data transmission is largely unproblematic, to date, for the more labor-intensive industries in the developing world.

Host government environmental controls shows up as a moderate concern, with a fairly even balance between responses at both ends of the spectrum. While 24 percent of the respondents judge such controls, or their absence, as negligible in their cost-related investment decisions, 13 percent find them critical. Seventy percent of those companies for which environmental controls present a critical expenditure are producers of either chemicals, oil, or minerals—industries which clearly have a high risk of deleterious effects on the local environment.

Host government environmental controls are likely to take on an increasing significance for international business in the 1990s. In light of increased global warming, toxic wastes, acid rain, and general environmental deterioration, LDCs are beginning to consider more seriously imposing and enforcing environmental controls. At the time of writing, Indonesia has just brought its first case under an environmental law against a factory in East Java—a decision which could have far-reaching repercussions for not only domestic but foreign enterprises.

In addition, some institutions engaged in debt-equity swap arrangements, notably in Brazil and some African countries, are investing in environmental projects, so will presumably be taking a keen interest in their success. (For more on debt-equity swaps, see de Vries, chapter four).

Focus on this concern is also augmented by the fact that both environmental and debt-related issues, as they pertain to Third World economic development, appear for the first time as high priority agenda items for the 1989 Paris economic summit of the Group of Seven (G-7) leading industrialized countries.

Government Action

With regard to what single U.S. government action would have the greatest impact on FDI cost reduction, the high-priority given to tax policies, expressed first in the "market entry" section, is repeated here. Fifty-four percent of the respondents to the "cost of FDI" government-action question singled out more favorable tax treatment at home. In fact, in this section better tax treatment is mentioned *four times* as frequently as the nearest contender: improved financing terms/lower cost of capital. (This rises to 12 *times* as often under "return on FDI.")

Since tax concerns expressed in the "cost" section largely overlap with those in the "return" section, they will be treated together here in order to give a more comprehensive view. The tax considerations elaborated in these two sections basically fall into two categories: (1) tax credits and (2) preferential tax treatment and incentives to spur Third Word development, as amplified below. In addition, tax code compatibility of home and host is mentioned as a desired end in the "market entry" section.

(1) *Tax credits.* Many see the need for a more beneficial foreign tax credit scheme. Along with proposals for greater foreign tax/investment credits are specific suggestions involving the reduction or removal of tax credit restrictions. These include new limitations on FTC (Federal Trade Commission) utilization, and the current interpretation of IRS regulations as applied to Section 902. Under Section 902 of the Internal Revenue Code as presently interpreted, for example, U.S. shareholders in Saudi Arabian limited liability companies are denied full credit for income taxes paid to the Saudi government.

One company labeled as counterproductive to foreign investment the requirement to calculate foreign tax credits based on receiving foreign income in separate "baskets." This also results in taxing "passive" income in certain foreign affiliates for U.S. tax purposes. Another indicated that more favorable tax treatment for LDC investments should include steps to allow greater use of excess foreign tax credits and the ending of interest allocation to assets in LDCs.

There was also mention of negotiating more double tax treaties, and eliminating imputed taxes for royalties not permitted by the host.

(2) *Preferential tax treatment for LDC development.* Some companies communicated their desire for preferential tax treatment, including incentives such as short-term tax relief, for income earned in less developed, capital-deficient countries. Others expressed the need for tax breaks/deductability during the initial stages of the investment, to counteract start-up losses and other early development expenditures.

A number of companies recommended tax rebates or other incentives associated with Third World investing that would foster "trade not aid," and generally emphasized the role private enterprise could play in Third World development if increased government incentives were instituted. One respondent stated this in terms of discouraging "forms of aid to host governments which in effect supplant what would be available from private enterprises on a negotiated basis."

After tax grievances, as mentioned above, many corporations expressed the desire for improved financing terms and lower cost of capital (15 percent of the companies responding to this question). Other suggestions for cost-related government action can be grouped together, as in the "market entry" section, as U.S. government non-interference, and the promotion of free trade. A number of other corporations expressed the need for U.S. pressure to eliminate LDC performance requirements, and the protection of intellectual property rights. In addition, one company specifically suggested government grants for training foreign locals.

Section IV: Return on FDI

Critical Factors

The factor most frequently rated critical where return on investment is concerned is *projected market growth* (by 61 percent of the respondents). Interestingly, *market size,* judged critical by over half (53 percent) of the participants, nonetheless falls well down the ranked list, in sixth place. This reaffirms the findings from Section I that companies are primarily preoccupied with positioning themselves for the future.

A very close second in importance to highest-ranked projected market growth is a familiar theme from the two preceding sections: tax policies of home and host. Here again, well over half of the respondents ranked tax policies as critical. Sixty percent consider *host government tax policies* critical to their return on investment; 53 percent find *U.S. tax policy* a critical concern. Host government tax policy and U.S tax policy are almost unanimously considered moderate-to-critical factors in the investment decision-making process where investment return is concerned. A mere 1 percent of the participants deemed host tax policy negligible in this category, and only 4 percent found U.S. tax policy a negligible factor.

Nearly as critical as host tax policies and future growth of the market are *host pricing controls* and *foreign exchange rates and controls on transfers,* both so ranked by 58 percent of the respondents. As noted earlier (footnote 4, *supra*), indications are that while these two exchange-related factors are combined in both this and the "cost" sections, it is the exchange controls, rather than the exchange rate fluctuations that pose the critical element.

Fifty-six percent of the corporations in the survey consider *competition* critical. Of the scant 9 percent that consider it a *negligible* factor, over half are in extractive industries (mining or oil). Such natural-resource-related industries are largely immune from many of the considerations that concern other more market-oriented industries. The fact that such companies are often operating under a government contract—or have reached some other kind of agreement with the host government—to extract certain reserves, also obviates the need to concern themselves overly with competitors.

The ranking of factor "criticalness" has been reported up to here based strictly on the data from the "critical" ratings. If the factor sensitivity is calculated on the basis of "weighted" values that take into consideration the "moderate" and "negligible" responses as well as the "critical," the order of the ranking may be altered. (See Appendix D-2 for range of weighted formulae applied.)

This weighted approach proves especially interesting here in the "return on FDI" section. For example, on a weighted basis, host tax policy ranks most critical and projected market growth—given the relatively high percentage of respondents that consider it a negligible factor—drops to the third most critical return factor (Cp. graphs: Appendices D-3 and D-4.)

The same phenomenon occurs when comparing the critical rating of LDC market size and that of U.S. tax policy. Although six different "return" factors are more often mentioned as *critical* to the multinationals' LDC investment strategy than U.S. tax policies, five of them are also more often deemed *negligible*. The result again is that, on a weighted basis, U.S. tax policy jumps from the seventh most important factor to fourth, only marginally behind foreign exchange rates/controls on transfers, and projected market growth, with host tax policy moving into first place.

While the criticalness of tax factors is reaffirmed by applying the "weighted" analysis, market size (like projected market growth shown above) is *less* critical on a weighted basis, moving from sixth to seventh place. Given the significant number of companies judging it a *negligible* factor in their investment decisions, the weighted value for market size falls well below the other most critical factors. (Cp. graphs: Appendices D-3 and D-4.)

Some Observations on "Negligible" Return Factors

In investigating which types of companies from our survey sample find the above market-related factors (size and projected growth) *negligible*, out of the 13 percent of respondents that consider market *size* negligible, one manufactures just over the Mexican border for the U.S. market and another 60 percent are in extractive industries. Similarly, out of 13 percent (largely though not wholly synonymous with the above) that rated projected market *growth* in LDCs negligible, one is again the above-mentioned transborder company manufacturing for the American market, and another 70 percent produce oil and minerals.

That the factor most often mentioned as negligible with respect to return on FDI (by 47 percent) is *natural resource reserves* is obviously a reflection of the small percentage of overall survey respondents that are engaged in extractive industries. It also may be indicative of the substantial shift of MNCs from extractive industry orientation to consumer orientation. So it is not surprising that for most of the companies that did judge such reserves critical (23 percent), this factor is absolutely key to their successful operations. Three-quarters of these heavy industries rely on the availability of minerals, oil, or forests. Any other factor for such industries is secondary, and a factor like projected market growth can for them be virtually inconsequential.

Mandatory licensing of technology is another factor considered negligible by a significant number of multinationals (23 percent), with regard to return on FDI. One executive stated: "Know-how is what is important, not mandatory licensing of technology." Part of the explanation for the relatively high "negligible" rating, however, is that some of the participating multinationals are in relatively low-technology industries. Even so, more of the participants (38 percent) found this factor critical than found it negligible.

Government Action

More favorable tax treatment dominates as a recommended U.S. government action for both cost and return considerations. In considering "return on FDI," the percentage of respondents judging tax issues critical jumps to 63 percent, which is exceptionally high for respondent-generated (write-in) answers. Tax-related responses appear *12 times* more frequently than the next most critical concern. Respondents' tax concerns are fully covered under the "Cost of FDI: Government Action" section, since, for this particular priority, "cost" and "return" responses largely overlapped.

Other suggestions for U.S. government action to enhance return on FDI include improved financing terms and the need for a more stable international exchange rate system, especially a stabilized U.S. dollar. This is a clear reflection of not only substantial G-7 fluctuations but also exchange rate volatility in some developing countries, where hyper-inflation is a corollary (especially true of certain Latin American countries).

Another concern equally expressed under "return on FDI" is the need to eliminate host government exchange controls and restrictions on capital movements. This brings us full circle to those same issues surrounding guaranteed remittance of earnings that tolled an overwhelming 81 percent of the "critical" vote with regard to initial market entry decisions. We have already elaborated on this earlier in the analysis, and there is no need for further commentary.

Summary and Conclusions

Investment Insurance

While our survey confirms and perpetuates earlier findings that economic risks outweigh political risks in investment decisions, it does show a shift away from the notion that political risk *per se* has virtually ceased to be a serious deterrent to FDI in the Third World. Combining the responses in Section I on insurance and on reasons for increasing/decreasing investments, with those in Section II on political risk and threat of expropriation, two main points emerge.

First, the earlier emphasis on political risk assessment, which proved highly unreliable and gave way to political risk management, seems in so doing to have diminished and in some cases even obviated the need to rely on insuring the risk at all. And second, there appears to be a move away from investing in high risk regions rather than a move toward relying on insurance to mitigate risk.

For these and other reasons, the cost-effectiveness of existing schemes is clearly called into question by our survey findings, though OPIC still insures the lion's share of the 26 percent of our respondent companies that do hold investment insurance and has the interest of an additional 8 percent who plan to insure with OPIC in future.

MIGA may be a partial solution, and the interest shown by the respondents in this new program indicates that there is clearly such a need.

Meanwhile, the most effective "insurance" at the present time seems to be (1) learning to conduct multinational business operations as effectively as possible in the very midst of the political and economic environment as it develops; and (2) steering away from investing in high risk areas.

Home Government Policies

One quarter to one half of U.S. multinationals participating in our survey are either indifferent to or opposed to government involvement in their Third World direct investments. The primary concern for which these corporations do see home government action as desirable is in the area of more favorable tax treatment. Cumulatively, in all three categories analyzed ("Market Entry", "Cost of FDI", and "Return on FDI"), tax-related responses are far and away the single most predominant concern in considering foreign direct investments and/or in enhancing FDI benefits.

The particular types of tax reforms suggested are in the area of tax credits and tax incentives to encourage U.S. corporations to participate in Third World development through FDI. (Specific suggestions in this high-priority area are elaborated in the text under Section III: Cost of FDI: Government Action.)

Thus home-related concerns *per se* are largely associated with retention of earnings and, to a lesser extent, cost of capital, which is to be expected from profit-oriented undertakings.

Host Government Policies

For the most part it is barriers that originate with the host, particularly host government restrictions on remittance of earnings, that present more of a hindrance to Third World investment than policies originating at home. A close second to remittance policies are host state tax requirements.

In this regard, it is interesting to note that, in market-entry considerations, one quarter to one half of our sample favor a "hands-off" policy on the part of the U.S. government. Yet a significant 19 percent

171

specifically advocate U.S. government pressure or negotiation to reform some of the unfavorable host practices.

U.S. Government Action

If the U.S. government were to respond to the perceived needs of its multinationals according to the results of this survey, it would promote FDI in the Third World by refraining from legislation or other forms of government intervention that would interfere with the free-flow of private investment capital.

It would review any existing laws and policies that may be impeding MNC operations abroad (short of the necessary national security safeguards), with a view to the balance of interests at stake. It would specifically reassess the tax code and tax credit policies where MNCs are concerned, in view of promoting LDC-specific investing as an alternative to "trade and aid," in order to stimulate urgently needed Third World economic growth and debt servicing. It would review the cost-benefit ratio of OPIC and monitor the new MIGA insurance scheme, while assessing their effectiveness in the promotion of investments to the developing world and the distribution of benefits.

With further reference to the Third World, it would concentrate its efforts—as it is currently doing through the GATT negotiating process—on pressing for investment policy reforms in the *host*, paying particular attention to the matter of host guarantees of profit repatriation, the number-one host-originating preoccupation displayed by the survey respondents.

While giving attention to the above, it would concentrate on getting its own house in order with regard to the twin deficits.

It would foster cooperation between the different branches of government to coordinate a trade and investment policy that would give a clear signal—not only to Third World nations but also to its industrialized trading partners—that it is serious about providing a strong economic base for the range of international trade and investment activities so necessary to its own economic welfare and that of the community of free nations.

SURVEY QUESTIONNAIRE

(TABULATED)

FDI PROJECT

Phase Two

FOREIGN DIRECT INVESTMENT AND INTERNATIONAL CAPITAL FLOWS TO THIRD WORLD NATIONS: UNITED STATES POLICY CONSIDERATIONS

CONFIDENTIAL QUESTIONNAIRE

RESPONDENT COMPANY NAME (optional)

_____

COMPANY CONTACT FOR QUERIES (optional)

Name_____

Department_____

Telephone (_____)_____

FOREIGN DIRECT INVESTMENT SURVEY

BACKGROUND

The International Business and Economics Program of CSIS is conducting a major initiative to investigate and assess the most urgent aspects of both Third World and industrialized country developments in the increasingly strategic area of foreign direct investment.

In order to assure the broadest expression of genuine business interests, we are including in the study a survey on the most critical impediments faced by direct investors in developing countries. With our assurance of strictest confidentiality and anonymity, we want to make certain that the real problems faced by corporations such as yours, investing in Third World nations, come to the attention of key U.S. decision-makers in their ongoing policy considerations both at home and in the GATT.

We are anxious to include the market entry and/or operational difficulties encountered by your corporation in the findings of our survey. We feel it is an opportunity for you to anonymously express your most critical problems through a vehicle that can have direct policy impact.

You may also wish to enclose sundry reports or other relevant documentation already prepared by your company which would supplement the information you provide in the questionnaire.

Once again, in publicizing any of the survey results, we will of course observe the strictest confidentiality. Also, data will be so aggregated as to assure anonymity to any individual company.

Enclosed is a stamped self-addressed envelope for your convenience in returning the questionnaire. Please return all additional materials as well to:

Dr. Cynthia Day Wallace
Senior Fellow and Project Director
International Business and Economics Program
Center for Strategic and International Studies
1800 K Street N.W., Suite 400
Washington, D.C. 20006

If you would prefer to respond by phone or by personal interview, please contact Dr. Wallace's office at (202) 775-3178.

We would appreciate receiving your response by 15 July 1988, and thank you in advance for your cooperation in this effort.

I. YOUR COMPANY'S THIRD WORLD INVESTMENTS

A. MAJOR PRODUCT LINE(S) _____

B. TYPE(S) OF INVESTMENT (e.g. manufacturing facility, service industry, R&D lab) _____

C. INVESTMENT POSITION
1. Please give a brief description of the extent of your company's direct investments in Third World countries over the last three to four years, indicating countries or regions.

2. In which of these countries/regions is your FDI *increasing*, and what is the most significant reason for the increase?

3. In which of these countries/regions is your FDI *decreasing*, and what is the most significant reason for the decrease?

D. INVESTMENT INSURANCE
1. Do you now, or do you plan to, participate in the following investment protection schemes?

SCHEME	PARTICIPATION	
	Present	Planned
a. The U.S. Government's Overseas Private Investment Corporation (OPIC)	23.4%	7.8%
b. The World Bank's Multilateral Investment Guarantee Agency (MIGA)	0.0%	13.0%
c. The International Finance Corporation's Guaranteed Recovery of Investment Principal (GRIP)	3.9%	6.5%
d. Other _____	2.6%	2.6%

2. Have you ever participated in an insurance scheme and later withdrawn? If so, please explain briefly. (Attach additional pages if necessary.)

II. MARKET ENTRY

A.   The following factors, along with the continuing economic climate, can influence market entry for foreign direct investment. Please respond as to whether each is a *critical* factor, plays only a *moderate* role, or is a *negligible* factor in your company's investment decision process. Please place a check next to the appropriate item and briefly explain below.

FACTOR	CRITICAL	MOD–ERATE	NEG–LIGIBLE
Positive			
1. Guaranty of national treatment	34.9%	55.5%	9.6%
2. Protection from expropriation	76.4%	16.9%	6.8%
3. Guaranteed remittance of earnings	81.3%	18.7%	0.0%
4. Availability of dispute settlement facilities	25.7%	60.8%	13.5%
Negative			
5. Unwieldy host bureaucracy (unreasonable "red tape")	31.3%	62.7%	6.0%
6. Unfavorable investment laws	69.9%	30.1%	0.0%
7. Threat of war/hostilities	76.7%	19.2%	4.1%
8. Barriers to imports	44.0%	48.0%	8.0%
9. Imposition of export quotas	36.5%	48.6%	14.9%
10. Exchange rate fluctuations	25.3%	46.7%	28.0%
11. Exchange controls	37.8%	54.1%	8.1%
12. Corrupt practices	51.4%	44.6%	4.1%
13. Capital market regulations	12.0%	64.1%	23.9%
14. Other:			

B. What single U.S. government action would be most beneficial to your company in facilitating market entry for FDI in LDCs?

If you have further comments, please use space below or attach separate page(s).

III. COST OF FDI

A. The following factors influence the costs associated with foreign direct investment. Please respond as to whether each is a *critical* factor, plays only a *moderate* role, or is a *negligible* factor in your company's investment decision process.

FACTOR	CRITICAL	MOD–ERATE	NEG-LIGIBLE
1. Cost of capital	36.2%	49.3%	14.5%
2. Availability & costs of raw materials & resources	44.7%	36.8%	18.4%
3. Availability & cost of trained labor	42.1%	47.4%	10.5%
4. Availability of advanced communications, informatics & production technologies	14.5%	64.5%	21.1%
5. Transportation costs	27.6%	52.6%	19.7%
6. Host productivity	29.3%	57.3%	13.3%
7. Impact of foreign exchange fluctuations or controls	37.7%	59.7%	2.6%
8. Impact of new investment on costs of existing production	23.9%	54.9%	21.1%
9. Host government policies which affect costs of FDI:			
a. environmental controls	13.2%	63.2%	23.7%
b. trade policies	29.3%	54.7%	16.0%
c. industrial relations policies	17.8%	67.8%	14.5%
d. performance requirements	27.3%	58.4%	14.3%
e. foreign exchange policies.	49.3%	46.7%	3.9%
f. remittance policies	73.1%	25.0%	1.9%
g. tax law and policies	64.5%	33.6%	2.0%
h. ownership percentage requirements	63.9%	33.5%	2.5%
i. illicit practices	52.6%	42.1%	5.3%
j. unfair competition policies	39.7%	49.3%	11.0%
k. barriers to transborder data flows	24.0%	49.3%	26.7%

(Continued on next page)

10. U.S. government policies which
    affect costs of FDI:

a. trade policies	30.3%	50.0%	19.7%
b. industrial relations policies	7.3%	56.7%	36.0%
c. Foreign Corrupt Practices Act	25.0%	46.1%	28.9%
d. tax laws	63.6%	33.8%	2.6%

11. Other:

B. What single U.S. government action would be the most effective in decreasing the cost of FDI for your company in LDCs?

If you have further comments, please use space below or attach separate page(s).

IV. RETURN ON FDI

A. The following factors influence the expected return on foreign direct investment. Please respond as to whether, in your primary product line, each is a *critical* factor, plays only a *moderate* role, or is a *negligible* factor in your company's investment decision process.

FACTOR		CRITICAL	MOD–ERATE	NEG–LIGIBLE
1.	Market size	53.3%	33.3%	13.3%
2.	Natural resource reserves	22.7%	30.7%	46.7%
3.	Projected market growth	61.3%	25.3%	13.3%
4.	Tax policies of home government	52.6%	43.4%	3.9%
5.	Tax policies of host government	60.0%	38.7%	1.3%
6.	Competition	56.0%	34.7%	9.3%
7.	Mandatory licensing of technology	37.7%	39.0%	23.3%
8.	Pricing controls	58.1%	30.4%	11.5%
9.	Foreign exchange rates & controls on transfers	57.9%	36.8%	5.3%
10.	Controls on charges for management fees & technology.	31.1%	51.4%	17.6%
11.	Effect of new investment on existing operation	22.5%	53.5%	23.9%
12.	Investment incentives	27.7%	66.9%	5.4%

B. What single U.S. government action would most enhance your company's return on FDI in LDCs?

If you have further comments, please use space below or attach separate page(s).

V. FDI IN INDUSTRIALIZED NATIONS

1. Would your company benefit from a similar survey geared to targeting major corporate concerns in FDI-related activities between industrialized nations? YES_____ NO___

2. If YES, please indicate your area(s) of interest:

a. _____ JAPAN (in light of reciprocity considerations, productivity, etc.)

b. _____ EUROPE (with a view to the 1992 integrated market, competitiveness, etc.)

c. _____ CANADA (in light of the new investment provisions of the Free Trade Agreement, etc.)

If you have further comments, please use space below or attach separate page(s).

APPENDIX B-1

MARKET ENTRY (II.A)

SERIATIM RANKING OF FACTORS

MOST CRITICAL	WEIGHTED AVERAGE
1 Guaranteed remittance of earnings	(1) Guaranteed remittance of earnings
2 Threat of war/hostilities	(2) Threat of war/hostilities
3 Protection from expropriation	(3) Protection from expropriation
4 Unfavorable investment laws	(4) Unfavorable investment laws
5 Corrupt practices	(5) Corrupt practices
6 Barriers to imports	(6) Barriers to imports
7 Exchange controls	(7) Exchange controls
8 Imposition of export quotas	(9) Guaranty of national treatment
9 Guaranty of national treatment	(10) Unwieldy host bureaucracy
10 Unwieldy host bureaucracy	(8) Imposition of export quotas
11 Availability of dispute settlement facilities	(11) Availability of dispute settlement facilities
12 Exchange rate fluctuations	(12) Exchange rate fluctuations
13 Capital market regulations	(13) Capital market regulations

NOTE: The left-hand column ranks the most critical factors on the basis of critical responses only. (See graph: Appendix B-3.) The right-hand (weighted) column represents the average of a range of weighting factors, attributing different sets of values to "critical," "moderate," and "negligible" responses. (See Appendix B-2 and graph: Appendix B-4.)

MARKET ENTRY (II.A)

SENSITIVITY ANALYSIS

	Critical	Moderate	Negligible	Weighted 6C+4M+1N	Weighted 6C+3M+1N	Weighted 6C+2M+1N	Weighted 8C+2M-2N	Weighted 6C+2M-2N	Weighted 4C+2M-2N	Average 6/2.5/-.5
RemittPols	81.3	18.7	0.0	562.6	543.9	525.2	687.8	525.2	362.6	534.6
War/Hostil	76.7	19.2	4.1	541.1	521.9	502.7	643.8	490.4	337.0	506.2
Exproption	76.4	16.9	6.8	532.8	515.9	499.0	631.4	478.6	325.8	497.3
UnfavrLaws	69.9	30.1	0.0	539.8	509.7	479.6	619.4	479.6	339.8	494.7
CorrptPrac	51.4	44.6	4.1	490.9	446.3	401.7	492.2	389.4	286.6	417.9
ImportBars	44.0	48.0	8.0	464.0	416.0	368.0	432.0	344.0	256.0	380.0
ExchContrl	37.8	54.1	8.1	451.3	397.2	343.1	394.4	318.8	243.2	358.0
ExprtQuots	36.5	48.6	14.9	428.3	379.7	331.1	359.4	286.4	213.4	333.1
NatlTrtmnt	34.9	55.5	9.6	441.0	385.5	330.0	371.0	301.2	231.4	343.4
Bureaucrcy	31.3	62.7	6.0	444.6	381.9	319.2	363.8	301.2	238.6	341.6
DisputeSet	25.7	60.8	13.5	410.9	350.1	289.3	300.2	248.8	197.4	299.5
ExchFlctns	25.3	46.7	28.0	366.6	319.9	273.2	239.8	189.2	138.6	254.6
CapMktRegs	12.0	64.1	23.9	352.3	288.2	224.1	176.4	152.4	128.4	220.3

NOTE: The above table attributes different sets of values to 'critical,' 'moderate,' and 'negligible' responses based on response percentages. The formula 6C+4M+1N, for example, indicates that the 'critical' response percentages were assigned a value of six, 'moderate' response percentages were assigned a value of four, and 'negligible' response percentages were assigned a value of one. The sum of the three parts yields the number shown in the column. The final column shows the average of the complete range of weighting formulae, and the reordered ranking appears in graph form in Appendix B-4.

MARKET ENTRY (II.A)

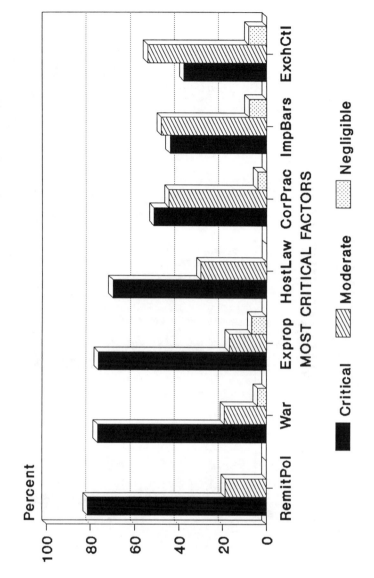

MARKET ENTRY (II.A)

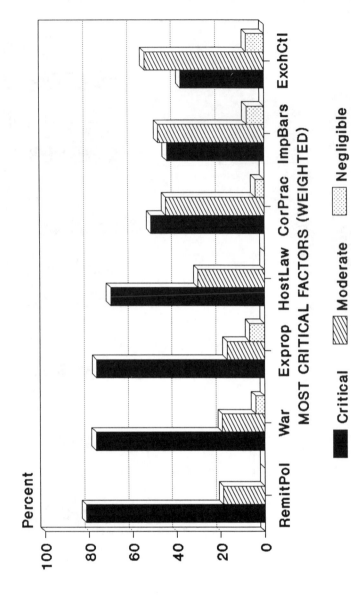

APPENDIX C-1

COST OF FDI (III.A)

SERIATIM RANKING OF FACTORS

MOST CRITICAL	WEIGHTED AVERAGE
1 Host remittance policies	(1) Host remittance policies
2 Host tax law and policies	(2) Host tax law and policies
3 Host ownership percentage requirements	(3) Host ownership percentage requirements
4 U.S. tax laws	(4) U.S. tax laws
5 Host government illicit practices	(5) Host government illicit practices
6 Host foreign exchange policies	(6) Host foreign exchange policies
7 Availability & costs of raw materials & resources	(10) Impact of foreign exchange fluctuations or controls

8 Availability & cost of trained labor	(8) Availability & cost of trained labor
9 Host unfair competition policies	(9) Host unfair competition policies
10 Impact of foreign exchange fluctuations or controls	(7) Availability & costs of raw materials & resources
11 Cost of capital	(11) Cost of capital
12 U.S. trade policies	(13) Host productivity
13 Host productivity	(14) Host trade policies
14 Host trade policies	(16) Host performance requirements
15 Transportation costs	(12) U.S. trade policies
16 Host performance requirements	(15) Transportation costs
17 Foreign Corrupt Practices Act	(19) Impact of new investment on costs of existing production
18 Host barriers to transborder data flows	(20) Host industrial relations policies
19 Impact of new investment on costs of existing production	(18) Host barriers to transborder data flows
20 Host industrial relations policies	(17) Foreign Corrupt Practices Act
21 Availability of advanced communications, informatics & production technologies	(21) Availability of advanced communications, informatics & production technologies
22 Host environmental controls	(22) Host environmental controls
23 U.S. industrial relations policies	(23) U.S. industrial relations policies
See note on next page	

NOTE: The left-hand column ranks the most critical factors on the basis of critical responses *only*. (See graph: Appendix C-3.) The right-hand (weighted) column represents the average of a range of weighting factors, attributing different sets of values to "critical," "moderate," and "negligible" responses. (See Appendix C-2 and graph: Appendix C-4.)

COST OF FDI (III.A)

SENSITIVITY ANALYSIS

	Critical	Moderate	Negligible	Weighted 6C+4M+1N	Weighted 6C+3M+1N	Weighted 6C+2M+1N	Weighted 8C+2M-2N	Weighted 6C+2M-2N	Weighted 4C+2M-2N	Weighted Average 6/2.5/-.5
RemittPols	73.1	25.0	1.9	540.5	515.5	490.5	631.0	484.8	338.6	500.2
HostTaxLaw	64.5	33.6	2.0	523.4	489.8	456.2	579.2	450.2	321.2	470.0
Ownership%	63.9	33.5	2.5	519.9	486.4	452.9	573.2	445.4	317.6	465.9
US TaxLaws	63.6	33.8	2.6	519.4	485.6	451.8	571.2	444.0	316.8	464.8
IllctPrcts	52.6	42.1	5.3	489.3	447.2	405.1	494.4	389.2	284.0	418.2
FrnExchPol	49.3	46.7	3.9	486.5	439.8	393.1	480.0	381.4	282.8	410.6
RawMaterls	44.7	36.8	18.4	433.8	397.0	360.2	394.4	305.0	215.6	351.0
AvailLabor	42.1	47.4	10.5	452.7	405.3	357.9	410.6	326.4	242.2	365.9
UnfairComp	39.7	49.3	11.0	446.4	397.1	347.8	394.2	314.8	235.4	356.0
ExFlct/Ctl	37.7	59.7	2.6	467.6	407.9	348.2	415.8	340.4	265.0	374.2
CostCapitl	36.2	49.3	14.5	428.9	379.6	330.3	359.2	286.8	214.4	333.2
USTradePol	30.3	50.0	19.7	401.5	351.5	301.5	303.0	242.4	181.8	297.0
HostProdct	29.3	57.3	13.3	418.3	361.0	303.7	322.4	263.8	205.2	312.4
HostTrPols	29.3	54.7	16.0	410.6	355.9	301.2	311.8	253.2	194.6	304.6
TranspCost	27.6	52.6	19.7	395.7	343.1	290.5	286.6	231.4	176.2	287.3
PerfrmReqs	27.3	58.4	14.3	411.7	353.3	294.9	306.6	252.0	197.4	302.7
F.C.P. Act	25.0	46.1	28.9	363.3	317.2	271.1	234.4	184.4	134.4	250.8
TBDFBarier	24.0	49.3	26.7	367.9	318.6	269.3	237.2	189.2	141.2	253.9
NewInvstmt	23.9	54.9	21.1	384.1	329.2	274.3	258.8	211.0	163.2	270.1
HoIndstRel	17.8	67.8	14.5	392.5	324.7	256.9	249.0	213.4	177.8	269.1
AvailTelec	14.5	64.5	21.1	366.1	301.6	237.1	202.8	173.8	144.8	237.7
Environmnt	13.2	63.2	23.7	355.7	292.5	229.3	184.6	158.2	131.8	225.4
USIndstRel	7.3	56.7	36.0	306.6	249.9	193.2	99.8	85.2	70.6	167.5

NOTE: The above table attributes different sets of values to 'critical,' 'moderate,' and 'negligible' responses, based on response percentages. The formula, 6C+4M+1N, for example, indicates that the 'critical' response percentages were assigned a value of six, 'moderate' response percentages were assigned a value of four, and 'negligible' response percentages were assigned a value of one. The sum of the three parts yields the number shown in the column. The final column shows the average of the complete range of weighting formulae, and the reordered ranking appears in graph form in Appendix C-4.

189

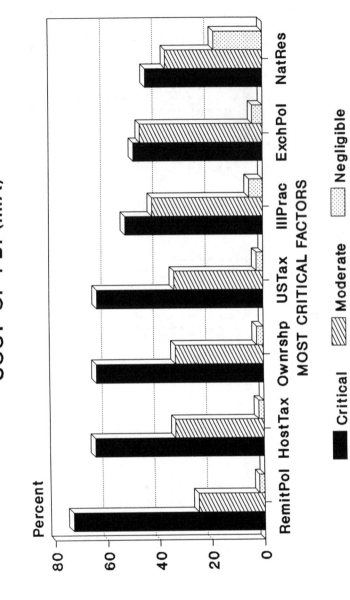

COST OF FDI (III.A)

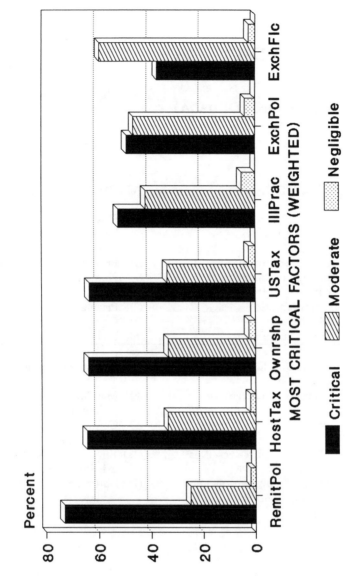

COST OF FDI (III.A)

APPENDIX D-1

RETURN ON FDI (IV.A)

SERIATIM RANKING OF FACTORS

MOST CRITICAL	WEIGHTED AVERAGE
1 Projected market growth	(2) Host tax policies
2 Host tax policies	(4) Foreign exchange rates & controls on transfers
3 Pricing controls	(1) Projected market growth
4 Foreign exchange rates & controls on transfers	(7) Home tax policies
5 Competition	(3) Pricing controls
6 Market size	(5) Competition
7 Home tax policies	(6) Market size
8 Mandatory licensing of technology	(10) Investment incentives
9 Controls on charges for management fees & technology	(8) Mandatory licensing of technology
10 Investment incentives	(9) Controls on charges for management fees & technology
11 Natural resource reserves	(12) Effect of new investment on existing operation
12 Effect of new investment on existing operation	(11) Natural resource reserves

NOTE: The left-hand column ranks the most critical factors on the basis of critical responses *only*. (See graph: Appendix D-3.) The right-hand (weighted) column represents the average of a range of weighting factors, attributing different sets of values to "critical," "moderate," and "negligible" responses. (See Appendix D-2 and graph: Appendix D-4.)

APPENDIX D-2

RETURN ON FDI (IV.A)

SENSITIVITY ANALYSIS

	Critical	Moderate	Negligible	Weighted 6C+4M+1N	Weighted 6C+3M+1N	Weighted 6C+2M+1N	Weighted 8C+2M-2N	Weighted 6C+2M-2N	Weighted 4C+2M-2N	Average 6/2.5/-.5
PjtdMktGth	61.3	25.3	13.3	482.3	457.0	431.7	514.4	391.8	269.2	424.4
HostTaxPol	60.0	38.7	1.3	516.1	477.4	438.7	554.8	434.8	314.8	456.1
PricCntrls	58.1	30.4	11.5	481.7	451.3	420.9	502.6	386.4	270.2	418.9
ExchCntrls	57.9	36.8	5.3	499.9	463.1	426.3	526.2	410.4	294.6	436.8
Cmpetition	56.0	34.7	9.3	484.1	449.4	414.7	498.8	386.8	274.8	418.1
MarketSize	53.3	33.3	13.3	466.3	433.0	399.7	466.4	359.8	253.2	396.4
HomeTaxPol	52.6	43.4	3.9	493.1	449.7	406.3	499.8	394.6	289.4	422.2
LicensTech	37.7	39.0	23.3	405.5	366.5	327.5	333.0	257.6	182.2	312.1
MgtTechFee	31.1	51.4	17.6	409.8	358.4	307.0	316.4	254.2	192.0	306.3
InvstIncnt	27.7	66.9	5.4	439.2	372.3	305.4	344.6	289.2	233.8	330.8
NatlResvs	22.7	30.7	46.7	305.7	275.0	244.3	149.6	104.2	58.8	189.6
NewInvstmt	22.5	53.5	23.9	372.9	319.4	265.9	239.2	194.2	149.2	256.8

NOTE: The above table attributes different sets of values to 'critical,' 'moderate,' and 'negligible' responses, based on response percentages. The formula 6C+4M+1N, for example, indicates that the 'critical' response percentages were assigned a value of six, 'moderate' response percentages were assigned a value of four, and 'negligible' response percentages were assigned a value of one. The sum of the three parts yields the number shown in the column. The final column shows the average of the complete range of weighting formulae, and the reordered ranking appears in graph form in Appendix D-4.

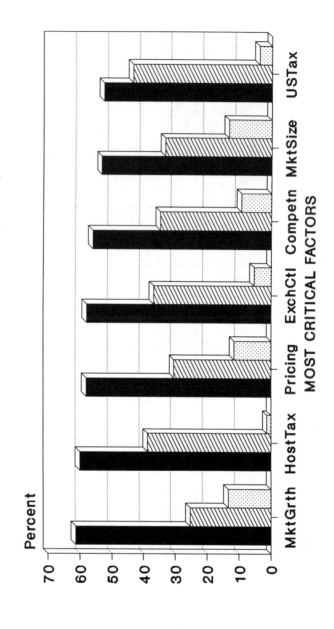

APPENDIX D-3

RETURN ON FDI (IV.A)

RETURN ON FDI (IV.A)

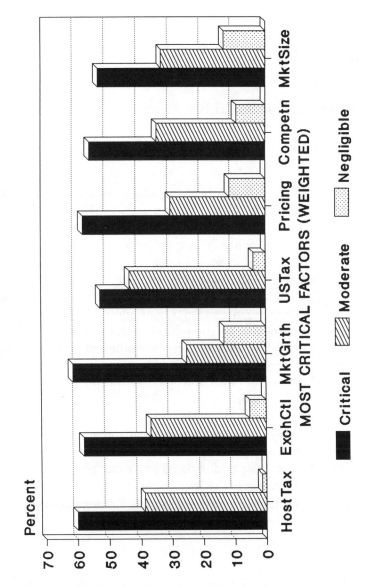

APPENDIX E-1

MARKET ENTRY (II.B)

RECOMMENDED GOVERNMENT ACTION

What single U.S. government action would be most beneficial to your company in facilitating market entry for FDI in LDCs?

1.	Non-intervention/non-interference	25%
3.	More favorable tax treatment	23%
3.	Improved U.S. trade policies	23%
5.	Encouraging host government to allow freedom of capital movements/investment repatriation	8%
5.	Strengthening intellectual property rights	8%
5.	Pressing for market access/relaxation of licensing constraints	8%
8.	Government protection against expropriation and other political risks	6%
8.	Accelerating the bilateral investment treaty process	6%
8.	Pressing for reciprocal treatment abroad	6%
11.	Improved financing terms/lower U.S. interest rates	4%
11.	Discouraging trade-related and other performance requirements in LDCs	4%
11.	Supporting U.S. business as part of foreign policy	4%
14.	Other	15%

NOTE: Responses have been summarized into 13 categories. Some responses included concerns that fall into more than one category, with the result that the percentages above total more than 100 percent. For the purposes of the accompanying pie graph (Appendix E-2), the figures are adjusted proportionately to achieve 100 percent. Percentages throughout, it will be recalled, are based on the number of actual responses to each given question.

MARKET ENTRY (II.B)

AREAS OF RECOMMENDED GOVERNMENT ACTION *

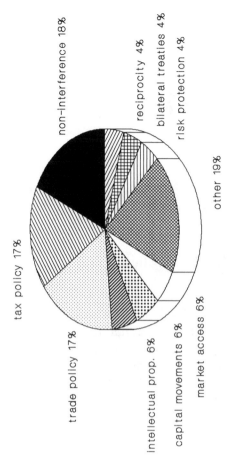

non-interference 18%

reciprocity 4%

bilateral treaties 4%

risk protection 4%

other 19%

tax policy 17%

trade policy 17%

intellectual prop. 6%

capital movements 6%

market access 6%

* See NOTE, previous page, regarding
discrepancy between percentages in graph
and percentages in text.

APPENDIX F-1

COST OF FDI (III.B)

RECOMMENDED GOVERNMENT ACTION

What single U.S. government action would be the most effective in decreasing the cost of FDI for your company in LDCs?

1. More favorable tax treatment	54%
2. Improved financing terms/lower cost of U.S. capital	15%
3. Non-intervention/non-interference	8%
4. Promotion of free trade	6%
5. Protection of intellectual property rights	4%
6. Other	33%

NOTE: Responses have been summarized into six categories. Some responses included concerns that fall into more than one category, with the result that the percentages above total more than 100 percent. For the purposes of the accompanying pie graph (Appendix F-2), the figures are adjusted proportionately to achieve 100 percent. Percentages throughout, it will be recalled, are based on the number of actual responses to each given question.

COST OF FDI (III.B)

AREAS OF RECOMMENDED GOVERNMENT ACTION *

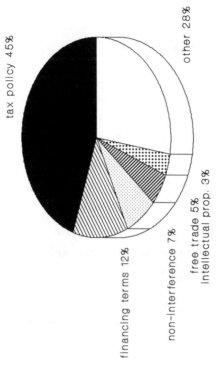

tax policy 45%

other 28%

financing terms 12%

non-interference 7%

free trade 5%
Intellectual prop. 3%

* See NOTE, previous page, regarding
discrepancy between percentages in graph
and percentages in text.

199

APPENDIX G-1

RETURN ON FDI (IV.B)

RECOMMENDED GOVERNMENT ACTION

What single U.S. government action would most enhance your company's return on FDI in LDCs?

1.	More favorable tax treatment	63%
2.	Improved financing terms	5%
2.	Promoting more stable exchange rates/stabilization of the dollar	5%
2.	Encouraging host governments to eliminate exchange controls and restrictions on capital movements	5%
5.	Other	29%

NOTE: Responses have been summarized into five categories. Some responses included concerns that fall into more than one category, with the result that the percentages above total more than 100 percent. For the purposes of the accompanying pie graph (Appendix G-2), the figures are adjusted proportionately to achieve 100 percent. Percentages throughout, it will be recalled, are based on the number of actual responses to each given question.

RETURN ON FDI (IV.B)

AREAS OF RECOMMENDED GOVERNMENT ACTION *

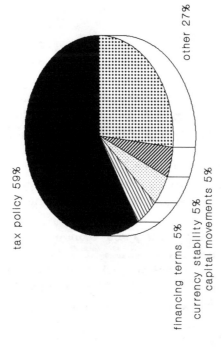

tax policy 59%

other 27%

financing terms 5%

currency stability 5%
capital movements 5%

* See NOTE, previous page, regarding
dicrepancy between percentages in graph
and percentages in text.

CONCLUSION

The economic well-being of a nation has become inexorably linked with international leadership and security. It is more important than ever that the private sector and the policymaking community find that *juste milieu* where, in a spirit of cooperation, they can achieve the underlying objectives of both, which is the highest common good. The process involves a mutual respect of goals that have the same fundamental premise: the perpetuation of the most stable and vibrant economy in the world, in the tradition of the free-flow of goods and capital, that will assure the security, strength and prosperity of all its inhabitants.

In the globally integrated economy in which we now operate, foreign direct investment offers one of those rare symbiotic relationships, economically, where all stand to benefit: the enterprise, the host country, and the home government. Wherever an opportunity exists in a friendly nation for outright aid, and government and international lending, to be substituted even partially by private initiative that lends to infrastructure enhancement and long-term growth, such ventures should be encouraged in every way. It is hoped that the present volume has substantially contributed to this end.

Cynthia Day Wallace

ABOUT THE CONTRIBUTORS

Harvey E. Bale, Jr. is Senior Vice President for International Affairs for the Pharmaceutical Manufacturers Association. Dr. Bale previously was International Public Policy Manager at Hewlett-Packard, dealing with international trade and investment issues. Prior to joining the private sector in 1987, Dr. Bale served in several capacities at the Office of the U.S. Trade Representative and the Department of Commerce. Among other assignments, he was a senior member of the U.S. Delegation to the Tokyo Round of Multilateral Trade Negotiations, and a senior U.S. delegate to the 1986 Punta del Este Ministerial meeting that launched the Uruguay Round of Trade Negotiations under GATT.

Dr. Bale has a Ph.D. in International Trade and Finance from the University of Maryland and has authored a number of articles on intellectual property and foreign investment issues. In 1986, he was awarded the Presidential Distinguished Service Award, the highest award given to career civil servants.

Rimmer de Vries is a Senior Vice President and Chief Economist for Morgan Guaranty Trust, and a noted international economist. He began his association with Morgan Guaranty in 1961, following five years as an economist with the Federal Reserve Bank of New York. Dr. de Vries is editor of *World Financial Markets*, which he founded in 1967. He has served on *Time* magazine's Board of Economists and on the Economic Advisory Board of the U.S. Department of Commerce. He is a member of the Advisory Committee of the Institute of International Economics; and a member of the Conference of Business Economists, and the Council on Foreign Relations.

Born in the Netherlands, Dr. de Vries obtained his B.A. from the Netherlands School of Economics. He earned his M.A. and Ph.D. at Ohio State University.

Clarke N. Ellis is Deputy Managing Director of the American Institute in Taiwan. Mr. Ellis was previously Director of the Office of Investment Affairs, Department of State. A career member of the Senior Foreign Service with the rank of Minister-Counselor, Mr. Ellis has served in Germany, Italy, Ethiopia, Switzerland and Taiwan, as well as in Washington, D.C., since becoming a diplomat in 1962. He received the Department of State's Superior Honor Award for his work on U.S. foreign investment policy.

Mr. Ellis received his B.A. in Government from the University of the Redlands; a Diploma in International Relations from the Bologna, Italy, Center of the Johns Hopkins School of Advanced International Studies; and an M.A. in Economics from the University of Michigan.

Donald L. Guertin is Senior Advisor on Public Affairs and a Director of the Atlantic Council of the United States. He is also a director of International Business Government Counselors, Inc., and a member of the State Department Advisory Committee on International Investment. Dr. Guertin's involvement in public affairs consulting follows a thirty year career at Exxon Corporation that culminated in a post as Senior Advisor on International Issues. Among his various capacities at Exxon, Dr. Guertin advised on and represented corporate positions on international investment and trade issues with the U.S. government and inter-governmental organizations, including the Organization for Economic Cooperation and Development and the United Nations. He has published widely in the fields of international investment and multinational enterprises.

Dr. Guertin holds an M.A. from the State University of New York at Albany and a Ph.D. in chemistry from the Rensselear Polytechnic Institute.

Theodore H. Moran is Landegger Professor and Director of the Program in International Business Diplomacy of Georgetown University, where he is currently concentrating on political risk analysis, corporate strategy, and techniques to offset political risk. Dr. Moran is also professor and member of the Executive Council of Georgetown University's School of Business Administration.

A former member of the Policy Planning Staff of the Department of State, Dr. Moran is widely known for his work on multinational corporations. In addition to some forty scholarly articles, he has published eight books, the most recent of which is *Investment in Devel-*

opment: New Roles for Private Capital, (Overseas Development Council, 1986). Dr. Moran has been a member of the Board or Advisory Committee of *International Organization, World Trade,* The Overseas Development Council, the Americas Society, and the American Political Risk Association.

Dr. Moran received his B.A. and his PH.D. from Harvard University.

Charles S. Pearson is Professor and Director of the International Economics Program at the School of Advanced International Studies, Johns Hopkins University. Dr. Pearson has taught or lectured at other institutions here and abroad. He is a member of the Johns Hopkins Foreign Policy Institute and the Reischauer Center for East Asian Studies at SAIS. He is also Senior Adjunct Associate at World Resources Institute.

In addition to numerous publications in the field, Dr. Pearson has been a consultant to the World Bank, the United Nations Conference on Trade and Development, the United Nations Commission for Latin America, the Organization for Economic Cooperation and Development, the U.S. Department of Commerce, the U.S. Joint Economic Committee, and to private industry and financial organizations. He also served as Senior Staff Economist for the Commission on International Trade and Investment Policy.

Dr. Pearson earned an M.A. in International Relations from Johns Hopkins, as well as an M.A. and Ph.D. in Economics from Cornell University.

Detlev F. Vagts is Bemis Professor of International Law at Harvard Law School, having also been associated with a New York law firm for five years previously. Formerly, he served as Counselor on international law with the U.S. Department of State. In addition to being Associate Reporter of the 1987 *Restatement on Foreign Relations Law of the United States*, Professor Vagts is author of major casebooks and other publications covering international business and multinational corporations, including "Coercion and Foreign Investment Rearrangements, 72 *American Journal of International Law* and "The Multinational Enterprise: A New Challenge for Transnational Law," 83 *Harvard Law Review*.

Dr. Vagts earned his undergraduate degree at Harvard College, as well as his LLB from Harvard Law School.

ABOUT THE EDITOR

Cynthia Day Wallace is a senior fellow in the International Business and Economics Program of the Center for Strategic and International Studies (CSIS) of Washington, D.C., and former Deputy Executive Director of the Investment Negotiation Program of the International Law Institute of Georgetown University Law Center. She has also been a fellow at the Max-Planck Institute of Private International Law in Hamburg and of Public International Law in Heidelberg, where she did research on foreign direct investment and taught in the Law Faculty of Heidelberg University. Dr. Wallace has also held academic posts at Harvard, McGill, Cambridge, and Columbia Universities and UN posts in Vienna, Geneva, and New York. She chairs an American Bar Association Subcommittee on International Codes and Guidelines for Multinational Corporations.

With a Ph.D. in international law from Cambridge University, Dr. Wallace is author and editor of a number of books on the subject of foreign direct investment and multinational enterprises, and her articles have appeared in journals and other publications dealing with international law and investment, in the United States and Europe. Her major work is *Legal Control of the Multinational Enterprise: National Regulatory Techniques and the Prospects for International Controls* (Nijhoff, 1983). Her most recent book is *Foreign Direct Investment and the Multinational Enterprise: A Bibliography* (Nijhoff, 1988).

INDEX

multilateral development banks (mdb) 15, 16, 26

Multilateral Investment Guarantee Agency (MIGA) 13-15, 24, 26, 99, 114, 118, 120, 130, 132-134, 137, 138, 153, 154, 161, 171, 172, 177

multilateral programs 4, 6, 24, 61, 63, 89, 90, 98, 99, 113, 118, 132, 148

multilateral trade negotiations (MTNs) 65, 79

multinational enterprises (MNEs/MNCs/TNCs) 2, 3, 4, 6-8, 19, 23, 25, 29, 31, 32, 37, 66-71, 85, 87, 96, 120, 129, 134-138, 147, 148

natural resources 6, 85, 91, 100, 106, 109, 117, 151, 152, 162, 163, 165, 169, 179, 181, 187, 190, 192, 193

national sovereignty 21

national treatment 9, 17, 21, 58, 111, 112, 123, 124, 126, 127, 129, 135, 136, 163, 178, 183, 184 (see also special and differential treatment)

Near East 39, 46

Netherlands 123, 126, 142, 146

New International Economic Order (NIEO) 22

newly-industrializing countries (NICs) 63, 65, 72, 150, 152 (see also East Asia)

Nicaragua 111

Nigeria 88, 90, 93, 94, 98, 99

non-discriminatory treatment 6, 99, 123, 124, 127, 146

non-intervention/interference 159, 160, 196, 198

non-tariff barriers 63

Norway 146

Organisation for Economic Co-operation and Development (OECD) 21, 23, 26, 71, 79, 80, 82, 120, 121, 126, 129, 130, 135, 138, 145, 148, 163

OECD Capital Movements Code 21

OECD Committee on International Investment and Multilateral Enterprises (CIME) 21

OECD Consultation Procedures 21

OECD Declaration on International Investment and Multinational Enterprises 129, 135, 138

OECD Declaration on National Treatment and Incentives and Disincentives to Investment 21

OECD Development Assistance Committee (DAC) 21

OECD Draft Convention on the Protection of Foreign Property 126

OECD Guidelines for Multinational Enterprises 3, 21, 26, 135, 136 (see also codes of conduct)

Office of Management and Budget 10

Overseas Private Investment Corporation (OPIC) 10, 13, 14, 20, 24, 26, 39-40, 46, 47-50, 52, 57, 58, 112, 113, 153, 154, 161, 170, 172, 177

ownership 4, 8, 10, 11, 29, 30, 44, 58, 62, 67, 68, 80, 85, 86, 96, 99, 100, 101

Panama 18

parallel lending 15, 16